M000112317

Lionheart:
The Real Life Guide
for Adoptive Families

Copyright © 2017 Big Love Family Projects

Published by Big Love Family Projects Pty Ltd
www.lionheartfamilies.com
The moral right of the authors have been asserted.

For quantity sales or media opportunities, please contact Jodie Hampshire, Publishing
Editor, at hello@lionheartfamilies.com

Cataloguing-in-Publication entry is available from the National Library of Australia.

ISBN: 978-0-6481168-0-6 (paperback)
         978-0-6481168-1-3 (ebook)

Publishing Consultant Linda Diggle, Book Boffin
Cover Illustration by Penelope Dullaghan
Cover Design by Studio 1 Design
Editing and Formatting by Author Secret

All rights reserved. Except as permitted under the Australian Copyright Act 1968
(for example, a fair dealing for the purposes of study, research, criticism or review),
no part of this book may be reproduced, stored in a retrieval system, communicated
or transmitted in any form or by means without written permission. All inquiries
should be made to the publisher at the above address.

Disclaimer: Although the authors and publisher have made every effort to ensure
that the information in this book was correct at press time, the authors and
publisher do not assume and hereby disclaim any liability to any party for any
loss, damage, or disruption caused by errors or omissions, whether such errors or
omissions result from negligence, accident, or any other cause.

How to Use This Book

So you have decided to adopt, or adopted already? We're guessing you're on a first-name basis with a psychologist, have a bookshelf bulging with how-to guides, and a blank journal ready to start your child's lifebook.

We did, too. Now, over a decade into our respective adoption journeys, we can tell you that just as important as the books, is the support of a village of parents who are stumbling down the same path as you.

For a golden two-year period in our lives, the three of us and our respective families were part of a small village of adoptive families in Dubai. We had two wonderful years of Wednesday afternoon playdates. They featured early supper for the children, and copious cups of tea dispensed with tissues, advice and hugs for the adults.

This book brings you short essays on a range of issues we've faced and the results of much reflection: what we have struggled with, where we have had success, and what we wish we'd known over the course of our journeys. This book is a synthesis of three families, a multitude of therapists and therapy sessions, and years of trial and error – all merged together and neatly written up for you in an honest and accessible way.

If you have a biological child, you have a shelf full of how-to books. You would have relied on them for reassurance as you saw change or wondered if something was normal as your baby grew.

Our intention is that this book will represent something of the same for adoptive parents. Between the three of us, we now have 12 children, both adopted and biological. When one of our adopted children has experienced a new issue, we've Googled or sought professional help; but most comforting has been the advice and reassurance we've gotten from each other, when we've checked in to see if any of the others have had similar experiences.

It may be difficult to relate to some of the stories in this book if you're early in your journey. Some of the stories may sound fanciful; you might think, "This isn't going to be us." You might wonder if we're exaggerating, or are a bit crazy. If we'd read this book pre-adoption, we would have discounted a lot of it. But the stories make more sense once you're home with your child. Read this book again when you're in the thick of things and we promise – we *promise* – you will have many "aha" moments.

We wish we'd had this book when we started out. We had lots of books, shelves full of books, but this content would have saved us years of misunderstanding our children, of struggling with a tricky issue until finally striking gold with a particular approach, of struggling generally.

The three of us collaborated on this book for a few reasons: to protect the specific stories of our children; to get the widest range of viewpoints we could on the issues we tackle; and because it gave us an excuse to chat, to write some of our memories down, and to fly to Singapore one weekend from our respective homes in Dubai, Sydney and near Melbourne to laugh, cry and write our way through to its completion.

Unusually for three adoptive families, none of us arrived at adoption through infertility. None of us are gay. None of us are especially religious. We each have families that mix adoptive and biological children. We understand that our experiences may be different to many of you who adopt. We each felt "called" to adopt – not through a religious devotion to service, but through a desire to love and parent a child in need of a permanent family. We are in no way qualified to deal with, and so do not speak about, the impact that infertility has on you as a parent. Your adoption counsellors will be able to direct you to helpful resources on this topic, if needed.

This book is firmly focused on the hard stuff. We assume that when things are rosy – and they so often are – the last thing you'll be doing is reading a parenting book. Don't take the content of this book as wholly representative of adoptive family life. Sure, it's bits of it, but there is plenty of offsetting, life-affirming wonderful stuff – we just haven't written it in here.

All of our adopted children were intercountry adoptions, some of the earlier sections speak more to this experience than to domestic adoption. We chose to adopt older children, special needs children, and sick children, as well as healthy babies. Whatever the makeup of our families and the backgrounds of our kids, we firmly believe the experiences we've had in parenting our children will resonate with other parents of adopted children, foster families, and children who have experienced trauma.

We have chosen to weave our individual experiences into short stories, each based on a theme. They're meant to be read when you need help with something specific; they're not telling a chronological story by any stretch. Some stories reflect the experience of one of us or our kids, and some are a mishmash of a few of us. We'll often use "I" to explain stories from the three of us, for ease of reading and for privacy.

There are five sections in this book:

◊ While our individual backstories don't provide much help to you as an adoptive parent, we find that people are always curious about why and how we adopted. Our real stories are in the **Prologue**.

◊ **The Early Days:** This section covers some of the issues you'll navigate as you complete the adoption process and bring your child home.

◊ **The Central Issue of Trauma:** Here we explain why trauma is significant to adoptive children, and delve into some of the issues that can stem from trauma, including attachment issues.

◊ **Different Behavioural Challenges:** This is the section I most wish we had had at the start of our journey – it would have saved us months or even years of angst. We explain some of the trickiest behavioural challenges we faced and what did and didn't work in improving them.

◊ **Therapy & Strategy Toolbox:** Oh, the multitude of therapies we have tried! This section is a distillation of what we've liked, from the expensive and complex, to the cheap-as-chips and simple (like chewing gum).

◊ **Parental Self-Care:** Any parent of any child needs to ensure they do what they can to stay calm and sane – easier said than done! Here we give some of our tips for coping when the days are rough.

We miss our Wednesday afternoons, but we were expatriate families in a specific place and time. Our friendships, though, endure and remain a first port of call when unexpected twists to our parenting journeys arise. We hope you find our stories honest and pragmatic, and that they give you the comfort of knowing that *yes*, this is normal, and *yes*, you and your child are going to be OK.

We've spoken for years about "doing something" in our children's birth countries. We've spoken for years about "writing something" to help other adoptive parents. Then we realised we should put the two together, meaning that all proceeds from Lionheart will go to Big Love Family Projects. You can learn more about these projects on our website (www.lionheartfamilies.com).

Jodie, Selina & Tammie

Foreword by Jodie Hampshire, Publishing Editor

This collection of stories has been years in the making: over a decade of parenting, and then a couple of years of putting these words down. Selina was enthusiastic from the start, and my request for stories had her writing pages and pages – it was something she'd meant to do for ages. Tammie started to think about what angles she could bring and started writing down some of her stories. For each of us, the process was intensely therapeutic.

I enthusiastically carved out twenty minutes here and there to write, but by the time I was breaking the halfway mark, I was struck with despair. One of my children was going through some serious issues, most certainly in response to the original trauma of family separation. I felt like a failure. What right did I have to write a guidebook to adoptive parenting when we were doing a terrible job at it? Despite very intense efforts to give our child security, safety, love, acceptance, professional support and understanding, we were still screwing up in a major way. We felt like a slow-motion car crash.

I spoke to Tammie on the phone as I returned home from a long day on a business trip. She asked me how this child was coping. I never like to talk a lot when we're in the midst of a storm; she knows me well, and got the message that things weren't great when I changed the subject quickly. She asked how the book was progressing. I said I had written and edited plenty, but felt I had no place giving advice to other adoptive parents when I was still learning very major lessons every day. It felt like all I could do was to tell people what *not* to do.

Then she said something that resonated with me, and motivated me to continue working on this book: "You are writing to help families build resilience. Shit will happen to all adoptive families; in fact, in all families. You get knocked over and you all get back up again. That is what you want to show people."

So here we are: mostly getting knocked down, but certain that we will continue as a family, and as individuals, to rise from the ashes again and again; grateful for each other most of the time, for this family I am both blessed and challenged to mother every day.

There are two things worth explaining about the book title. Firstly, the title of Lionheart. We wanted a word that described both the bravery and the love that all members of an adoptive family need to call upon, day in and day out. We threw ideas around, and liked "Braveheart" and "Lionheart". With four of our children being from Sierra Leone (which means "Lion Mountain" in Portuguese), Lionheart it was.

The second is the use of the word "real" in our book title. If you're anything like us, the use of the word "real" to describe your family, you as parents, or your child, is likely to slightly irritate you at the very least, if not downright offend you.

According to dictionary.com, real means "actually existing as a thing or occurring in fact; not imagined or supposed."

But with adoptive and foster families, the word is used lazily and loosely, in place of "biological" or "birth". We know people don't use it to cause hurt. We don't expect the average person to know appropriate adoption language, just like we sometimes stumble to sensitively use language with, say, a child with autism, because of our lack of knowledge.

But "real" is a word we need to out as totally incorrect to describe the relationships in our families. Selina's kids will sometimes guffaw when strangers ask them if she is their real mum: they'll giggle and say, "Well, she's not plastic!"

So yes, for all these reasons, we worried about using "real" in the title of our adoption guidebook. But we stuck with it. Because our aim is to deliver a book that is real, that describes lying and stealing and snot and pee, because that is what will be most helpful. We are adoptive parents parenting in real life. We are not therapists observing from a distance and writing about what we see. We live, breathe and (often don't) sleep our real stories. So real it is.

A word on the guest contributor, my husband, Robert Harris. My role in creating this book has been enabled through him. He bears the heavier parenting load in our family and has borne even more of it in recent months, with me regularly nipping upstairs to edit a chapter. Much of the progress we have made as parents has been made possible through his research, thought and unrelenting effort. The fact that we have survived and are starting to thrive in our parenting journey is testament to him. The healing we see in our children is testament to him.

Rob and Selina were both unhappy with the level of trauma-informed support available to adoptive parents, and have now studied childhood trauma. The section on Trauma was primarily their work.

To you all of you crazy mothers and fathers, with love.

Contents

To our adopted children: E, A, S, M, N and B.

I know you have been hurt,
I know that it has left scars.
That is OK.

I know some days I get it all wrong,
I yell when I should be hugging,
I talk when I should be listening,
And I let important moments go to waste.

Sometimes I am tired and impatient,
Sometimes I am frustrated – just like you.
Sometimes I have no idea what is happening inside you.
I want to. Believe me, I want to.

I want to understand you,
I want to know your thoughts, your feelings,
I want to know your truths.
But sometimes I know you don't know them, either.

And I want you to know this:
I will be here for you.
I can't take those yucky feelings away.
I don't want to change them.
I don't want to change you.
Everything you have been through up until this day
Has made you the person that you are.
And that person is great.

So, I sit and listen.
I sit and just be there.
No matter what is going on inside
Or what is going on outside.

I will show you hugs and happiness,
I will give you family and trust.
Most importantly, I will show you that I will love you.
No matter what.

Prologue: How Did We Get Here?

———◇———

"You're different. And I'm different too.
Different is good. But different is hard.
Believe me, I know."
Matthew Quick

———◇———

Jodie

Her name was strong and proud. She shared a birthday with my much-loved brother. She was beautiful, and while it seemed unthinkable to an overly-serious bleeding heart like me, her eyes were full of joy. And she was now waiting for us in a children's centre in Africa as we scrambled to arrange paperwork, visas, flights, clothes, toys and car seats.

Just six months earlier, we were living the life of young professionals in London, having moved there a year after our stormy, early summer Sydney wedding. I was finally working in the city at the centre of the universe: I had been waiting all my life to see the world. My husband agreed to put up with a stint in London, having emigrated from the UK some eight years earlier ("Seriously, you want to go back to work there? Do you know how cold and grey and…"). We had no pre-nuptial agreement, but this living-in-London deal was negotiated well before the wedding.

1

And then, London! I loved the street names and the everyday access to history and the black cabs whose drivers had encyclopaedic city knowledge and *The Guardian* on a Saturday and the tearoom at Liberty. I loved the proximity to Copenhagen and Barcelona and Istanbul. My workmates were confused when, for my thirtieth birthday, we went to New York for a few days and then Marrakech for a few more ("You don't understand," I said. "Sydney is so, so far away from everything!").

After two years, when they offered Robert a chance to head up the country office of a Dubai joint venture, he was keen to move on. "What's it like?" I wondered. "It's like a hot sandpit," he said with his characteristic dryness.

Off we went, sight unseen ("Act now, think later" is my *modus operandi*), and I went from hard-working professional to expat wife. In the serviced apartment we rented, I swam each day and overplanned how I wanted to decorate our new home. I found a Pilates teacher. I drank a lot of coffee. I was starting to consider looking for work, until I read a newspaper article that filled me with excitement. It was the story of a man I now call a friend, a British dad working in Dubai and parenting four gorgeous kids adopted from Africa. *You can do that?* Not in that country now, but in others, he explained. He was lucky, he said. I really thought so, too.

The seed had been sown on the issue of adoption before we'd gotten married. Robert had an adopted sister and a childhood filled with foster children coming in and out of his home. I had a desire to live life differently, and in my early thirties, I was still waiting for my biological clock to kick in and tell me I needed babies.

I remember distinctly a winter weekend on the south coast several months before our wedding, when we'd taken a case of different wines to try and select what we wanted to serve our wedding guests. Life was good; the sun had shone that Saturday and as we compared wines, we watched a documentary exposing the conditions of children living in Indian orphanages. It touched my heart like few things before it had. People often say they are called to do something, and in that hour, my heart and mind were galvanised and told me we needed to adopt. Like it was my purpose in life.

I spoke a mile a minute, excited. My husband had far more experience in this area and knew how hard things could be, and he was characteristically more circumspect in his consideration of my new and urgent calling. We discussed it at length, and finally agreed that this was something we wanted to do. The next day, we woke and still couldn't stop discussing our desire to become adoptive parents. We took a selfie with our digital camera to remember the day we made this decision.

We'd moved to London within a year of getting married, though, and two years later were living in the Middle East. We knew we were some years away from heading back to Australia, and were aware of how lengthy and frustrating the adoption process was at home. Age would not be on our side by that time, so we'd sadly put the adoption dream to bed, and went back and forth on whether we would have a family. Could we, even? I was scared to even try; it just never felt totally right. Perhaps I was afraid of disappointment, so I kept putting it off and off and off.

And now, I was not working, life was easy, and I had access to all these people who had adopted beautiful children. As I investigated further, I was stunned to realise it just might work. The calling I'd felt those years ago watching TV was reignited, and we were cautiously excited.

A flurry of paperwork, psych assessments, a couple of changes of birth country, photos and scant information on two beautiful children (you'll probably only bring one home, they correctly predicted) led to weeks of 3am email refreshing in the humid Arabian night, as we raced an imminent summer court closure and the prospect of a change in government sentiment post-election. One of those refreshes finally led to an email telling us, *Yes, come. Come.*

We realise now that our weekend away, when we had our initial conversation about adoption and agreed that was how we wanted our family to come together, was within days of our first daughter being born.

Selina

Always mature beyond my years, my determination, resilience and strong views were moulding me into a fiercely independent teenager. One strong view I'd always had was that I wanted to adopt one day.

In my early teens, I watched *The Dying Rooms*, a devastating undercover documentary, filmed in China by the BBC in 1993, that highlighted the impact of their one-child policy. As the credits rolled, I felt this compulsion to do something. I was 13 years old, and announced then and there that I would adopt a baby girl one day. My parents smiled, showed compassion and support as they always did, and left the subject to rest. I don't think they truly believed that, a little more than a dozen years later, they would be about to welcome their first grandchild into the family this way.

But my response to that programme was intense. The passion I had was powerful, and I knew this was not a passing thought. I knew from that moment that this adoption journey would be a path that I would travel one day.

After finishing university, I was working and playing hard in London. Routine bored me, and I was never bothered about adhering to social norms. When the opportunity arose for me and my almost-husband to move to Dubai for a sunshine-filled, tax-free expat posting, we both jumped at it. For those first couple of years, we were living the expat dream. Knowing my love of travel, and my emotional connection to the Chinese documentary I'd watched years before, my husband Billy booked a trip to China as a surprise Christmas present.

I see travel as an opportunity to experience the local culture, to visit places off the beaten track and learn what I can about the people of the land I'm visiting. After taking an overnight train from Shanghai to Beijing, we began talking to a British couple who'd arrived in China seven years ago to work in the oil industry. They'd lasted six months before giving up everything to care for special needs children on the outskirts of Beijing. We were invited to the centre and were greeted by the children, all of whom had special needs. They ranged from a little boy with hydrocephalus who was unable to lift his head, to a baby girl yellow with liver failure, to children with cleft palates and deformities. This couple had enabled over 300 surgeries for the children in their care, and we were fortunate enough to meet those waiting for surgery or being cared for in their final days. I walked away from our few hours with them totally drained, humbled, and crying my eyes out.

I knew then that we had to begin our adoption process upon our return to Dubai. It was March 2006, and little did we know that the little girl I'd dreamed of for over a decade was not in China, but about to be born in West Africa.

I'd always been very open with Billy about the prospect of adoption, and despite my now-overwhelming urge to start a family, I had no biological baby yearnings at this time. I was open to trying for biological children later, but my heart knew our first child must be my long-dreamed about adopted baby girl. To have found a man who respected this dream of mine, and who had now made it *our* dream, was special.

At home in Dubai, I read a newspaper article about a single British man who had recently returned from Sierra Leone with two beautiful children. We were two British expatriates, living in a foreign country, over 3000 miles away from "home". Was this really possible?

Kicking off our emotional and heart-wrenching adoption journey was my new obsession. The following week, I got the ball rolling and booked us in to the monthly Adoption Support Group meeting. Billy wasn't at all surprised or shocked at me being so gung-ho. He smiled, gave me a hug and said, "Let's do this!" We arrived straight from work, still dressed in our suits, apprehensive and nervous, and opened the door to a sea of beautiful adoptive families. I started to believe that this could actually happen.

We spoke to couples who had adopted from Guatemala, Cambodia, Thailand, Vietnam and Ethiopia, and met the man from the newspaper who had adopted from Sierra Leone. As soon as I got into the car, I burst into tears (again!). We hugged and, with tears rolling down my face, we didn't need to speak. We knew we had made the decision to move forward with our adoption journey.

At home that night, I was excited but nervous, not wanting to get too far ahead of myself (*This might really happen!*). We sat and talked until the early hours, and decided we had to find out more about the process. I couldn't sleep that night, tossing and turning as I imagined this little girl I had dreamed of for so long. I called the Adoption Psychologist the next morning, and we began the paperwork chase of stamps and documents. We kept ourselves busy with work, travel, moving house, planning a wedding and enjoying our expat freedom. Six months later, and only days after our huge Scottish wedding in the Arabian Desert, we received that referral email that would change our lives forever.

Tammie

On our second date, my now-husband and I decided we would adopt a child. Ridiculous. We were 18, had already decided we were madly in love after a week, and were convinced that we would one day be married and adopt a child.

We moved in together into a tiny one-bedroom apartment in Melbourne. One night, around a year later, I went off to a Plan International information evening on the AIDS epidemic in Uganda. The speaker was a doctor who was devastated by the number of children being orphaned by HIV. I listened intently, my eyes glued to this kind man's face. I took the brochures and sped home. As I raced through the door, I announced that we needed to get married right away so we could go to Uganda and adopt the children we had spoken about.

My patient husband looked up and met my intense stare with a kind smile: "Tell me about tonight, baby." I raced through the events of the evening and pled the case of the millions of children being orphaned in Uganda. "So we have to get married straight away so we can adopt some of these children," I told him. "They need loving homes *now*."

"OK," he agreed. "Let's get married soon, when we are ready, and then we will go and adopt some children." I knocked him over with the force of my hug. My mind was whirling with thoughts of adopting ten children. But how could we *only* adopt ten? We would need to adopt more…

We discussed the topic over and over for the next year. My rational husband ultimately convinced me to get married only when we were both ready.

We married two years later. I was very keen to start a family right away, and we were blessed with a daughter a year into our marriage. We then looked into adoption, and were devastated to find out the wait would be five to seven years. I didn't want to wait that long to add to our family, so we had a second daughter.

We were unable to get any closer to realising our adoption dream for the couple of years we then spent as expats in Qatar, where adoption is not possible. I had not given up, but wasn't sure if circumstances would ever allow us to fulfil it. We didn't know when we'd be living in Australia again, and we knew how hard it was to adopt and how long it took. Perhaps it would never happen.

Our next expat assignment was to Dubai. Not long after we arrived, I was walking in the mall with our two daughters when I noticed a white couple with an African baby. I stalked them for a bit, wanting to ensure she was, in fact, their child. Once I had convinced myself of that, I bowled up to them, so excited that the words all came spilling out too fast. *Oh wow! Did you adopt her while you were living in Dubai? I can't believe it! I'm so excited, we have been wanting to adopt for years. How do we do it?*

They were polite, but no doubt thought I was completely mad and took a few steps back. Being the helpful person that she is, and the advocate for adoption that all adoptive parents tend to become, the mother took down my number (she didn't hear my name properly, so stored me in her phone as "crazy mall lady"), and called me the next day to talk me through it.

This was the beginning of our crazy, emotional, amazing adoption journey, and the start of a beautiful friendship. Selina and I talked for an hour on the phone, and then she came over and we've continued to talk every day since. She introduced me to three other ladies, all going through adoption at the same time. Our little adoption village, that saw us through the paperwork, the waiting, the exhilaration, the sadness and the challenges, was born.

My husband and I giggled our way through the psychological assessments and home study, ploughed through the endless mountains of paperwork (needed from every country you have ever lived in!), and endured two devastating losses on our first two tries at adoption. Then we received the referral letter and photo of our son: our little baby boy.

The Early Days

———◇———

"Some of the most beautiful things worth having in your life come wrapped in a crown of thorns."
Shannon L. Alder

———◇———

Section Contents

Tell Me How
You Did It?

If you've spent any time at all looking into adoption, you won't be surprised by us pleading ignorance when it comes to current adoption laws and processes. It depends on your home country and your future child's birth country, and changes massively from year to year – month to month, even. A static book is no place to present this information to would-be adoptive families, when there are so many resources online devoted to keeping information current. And even if we wanted to, we were experts a decade ago, and what we knew then probably doesn't hold today.

The practicalities of our stories are that we are Australian and British nationals, and we adopted while living as expats in Dubai in the United Arab Emirates. In both Australia and the UK, it was (and, we believe, still is) possible to adopt as expats and then work with your home country to demonstrate that the adoption was legitimate, which then allowed you to apply for permanent visas and eventually citizenship for your child. This is not legal advice – goodness, no!

We will also say that, given our circumstances of long periods living abroad, it's likely that none of us would have been in our home countries at the right time to go through the adoption process. Being able to adopt was an unexpected blessing from our expatriate working stints, an opportunity that, for all of us, has been profound and life-changing, an opportunity that we are so grateful for.

So, now that we're clear that you need to do your own research into the process, here are some ideas:

◈ Find a support group or forum for people in your area who are preparing to adopt. Nothing beats the camaraderie of shared waiting, and it's a highly emotional time that can be hard for those who aren't in the same position to fully understand or appreciate. These people, whether real or virtual, will become fast friends – even if just for a limited period of time.

◈ Similarly, find groups or forums for people who are seeking to adopt from the same area as you, particularly if you are adopting from overseas. These people are likely to become firm friends, quite possibly for a lifetime. Some adoptive parents will be going to the country ahead of others, and will be able to report back on what to take, potential pitfalls, and the lay of the land more generally. I was fortunate to meet the children of a friend I'd made on one of our visits, before they even did. That was a bizarre situation, sure; but I considered it a privilege to give them a little cuddle.

◈ If you have access to adoptive parents in your area, do consider asking them if you can have a cup of coffee and hear about their experiences. Most adoptive parents are happy to have a truthful discussion with potential adoptive parents. We might get fed up with the two-bit questions of the curious, but we'll happily chat for hours with the serious. Just ask.

◈ This is also a good time to brush up on your adoption knowledge with a little reading. Some books that might help you in the beginning stages of your adoption journey are listed in the resources section of our website.[1]

---

1 www.lionheartfamilies.com/resources

Paperwork, Psychologists and Process

It was 7.30am on Thursday morning, and we were on our way to our first meeting with the social worker. My stomach churned as my husband kept assuring me that good things happen to good people; he was always trying to lighten the mood in a tense situation.

As we started chatting with the social worker, she quickly realised that I was the one driving this adoption discussion. She also saw that my husband was somewhat sceptical about the counselling process. After explaining the entirety of the procedure, the social worker turned to my husband with a question.

"I want you to imagine sitting at home with your daughter, now three or four years old, watching a film starring an African man. Your girl turns to you and asks: Is that my daddy? What are you going to tell her?"

He smiled and jumped to answer, stuttering and hesitating with an ill-considered sequence of thoughts. She stopped him quickly. She didn't really want an answer; she simply wanted him to think about whether he was ready to discuss racial issues, family reactions, stereotypes and the challenges of raising a black child in a white family.

Her point was taken. After that, he embraced every session, asking lots of questions where appropriate, and we supported each other through an emotional but rewarding couple of months.

Our final session involved the psychologist visiting our home to check its "child-readiness". I had heard that the psychologist liked to turn up early in the day, and sure enough, the appointment was booked for 7.30am on Friday (the first day of the Dubai weekend). I was up very early, lighting candles, putting on coffee and locking away our dog. I was feeling sick and hadn't slept well, but given the importance of this visit, I put on a cheery face. The psychologist came, inspected, and save a few comments on covering some wires, we were deemed "child ready". He signed our home study papers without hesitation.

That concluded the chatty, emotional part of the process. Now the paper chase began.

As the home study process came to an end, we ruled out China as we didn't meet the requirements (married for at least five years, over 30 years of age, etc.) and looked to Africa. We began our research and started with Sierra Leone, as the man we'd read about, who was now our friend, had adopted from there. We quickly found out that Sierra Leone had closed international adoptions (then reopened and closed them again), and so we started looking at similar countries and came across neighbouring Liberia (ranked the second poorest country in the world). I must admit that, despite being fairly widely travelled – having either visited or lived in India, America, the Caribbean, Europe, North Africa, Australia and the Middle East – I don't think I'd even heard of Liberia before, let alone been able to point to it on a map or tell you a fun fact about it.

We found the agencies that facilitated international adoption and landed on one in particular: they were honest, forthcoming with information, and said that as long as we dealt with the requirements on our side, they would do everything on the Liberian side.

We began our dossier. There was much negotiation, as they normally dealt with Americans and we just didn't have some of the requested information – there were no tax returns in our tax-free country of residence! We got there, though, and a month later had a pack of documents in hand: passport copies, birth certificates, references, home studies, bank statements, salary certificates, security checks, medical forms – you name it, we had it! We headed to every official building there was in Dubai to get as many official stamps as possible. That was it: we were done!

◆ ◆ ◆

Here are some tips for surviving what will be one of the most emotionally exhausting experiences of your life:

◊   Try and stay sane by treating your adoption process as a marathon, not a sprint. In all but the rarest of cases, it will take longer than you expect, and you will become consumed and exhausted by it. I haven't had another experience that really compares to it. The closest – and this comparison really goes nowhere near matching the emotional volatility and sense of time stopping as waiting to be referred a child – is the feeling of being in limbo when you've quit a job and are working out your notice period. You're still going through the motions in your old world, but all you can think about is the new world you're about to enter.

◊   Tick items off your "to-do" list and get some satisfaction from slowly pulling your dossier together. Gathering all the necessary documentation took us perhaps a month in all, so methodically complete the paperwork but try to stay balanced at this point. Make sure this isn't your only focus, as you will surely drive yourself mad. This is merely another step in the process, followed by the wait for referral, and then the wait to pick up. So it's actually more like a triathlon or pentathlon than a marathon.

◊   Set up electronic files, and keep scans and copies of everything. You will feel so relieved to be done that you'll never want to see those documents again, but stay disciplined: you are absolutely likely to need them again, and will be glad you were organised pre-adoption.

◊   Keep a balance of other things. If you're working, keep working.
Have other projects on the go, or you'll drive yourself mad. I
took a drawing class while waiting for our first child and that
was a wonderful respite from adoption obsession – none of my
classmates knew about our adoption plans, so I didn't have to
update them constantly. It was a breather from my otherwise
adoption-focused life.

◊   Distraction also works a treat. When you have zero control over
the timing of a situation, the only thing you can do is take your
mind off it. We went through the entire *Scrubs* box set during one
adoption, and *Six Feet Under* for another.

This is a process: follow it, and move to the next stage, my friend.

Referral

The moment you receive the call or email referral for your child is pure joy.

The dreaming, photocopying, counselling, worrying – it all stands still at this point. There is your child: in description, in name, in scant details, and, if you're lucky, in a photo.

This is the moment when you share your plans and your excitement with family and friends, if you haven't already. You bask in their excitement, and probably overshare information that you'll regret later (don't worry, we'll advise you on how to deal with intrusive questions, but it takes practice). You read and reread the email, or recount the phone call; you stare and stare at any photo you've been given. You dream about what this child might be like. How will it feel to hold them?

For closed(ish) adoptions, it's quite normal that your sadness for and about the family from which they have separated is delayed. In the referral stage, it's all magical thinking about your future life with your child. It's often not until later that you start thinking about the circumstances that led to their adoption, about any family they've left behind. None of us have a proper open adoption – we can only imagine the mixed feelings at the outset of the adoption process in these circumstances.

The good news is that you have a child waiting for you. The bad news is that there's still more waiting. And the waiting is even harder once you know who your child is.

To deal with this wait – which will feel like the longest of your life – apply the same techniques as we recommended in the paperwork stage. There are also some additional things you can do:

◈ Prepare your home for your new child. We'll cover this later, but with the benefit of hindsight, we think co-sleeping with a new child helps tremendously with bonding. We didn't do it with all of ours, thinking it more important to get our new child into a good sleep routine. But we wish we had. I've now co-slept with a child going through some challenges and it's made the world of difference to her. We did this for around nine months, and then we started to gradually phase her back into her own bed. Think about your bed and sleeping set-up. Perhaps put them into their own bed for a nap, but your bed at night.

◈ Decorate your child's room. This was one of the most joyful parts of the process for me: I loved picking out little prints for their walls, choosing bedcovers and toys, and imagining reading books in their rooms.

◈ Buy your child's clothes ahead of time. The centre will be able to tell you their current size, and keep in mind that it may surprise you. Many of our children were so much smaller than anticipated due to malnourishment. Again, this was one of my favourite parts. Certainly, when our daughter first came home, one of her favourite things to do was to open her wardrobe and look through her new clothes. You can easily find suggested shopping lists online.[2]

◈ Choose some beautiful toys and books for your child, and be conscious of having a variety of both. We have a list of our favourite books for our kids generally, and a list for adopted families especially, on our website.[3]

---

2 This one isn't over-the-top: http://www.parents.com/parenting/adoption/facts/adoptive-parents-shopping-list/

3 www.lionheartfamilies.com/resources

◇ If you are planning to have an adoption shower, do it now, before your child comes home. Too many toys will overwhelm your child as they aren't used to having lots of personal possessions. An alternative idea might be to ask for books instead. Reading to your child is awesome for bonding, even though they are likely to struggle to concentrate initially as they are unlikely to have been read to before.

◇ Print out some pictures of your home and environment, and even take a video, to show them when you meet them. We had a cheap little flipbook that we'd show the kids and tell them: this is a plane, this is our house, this is your room, this is your Nan, etc. You'll want to do all you can to reduce their fear of the unknown.

◇ Speak with the children's centre about what supplies they need. If family and friends are excited and want to buy gifts for your new child, consider asking them for items for the children's centre instead. Think about longevity: if you give soccer balls, include a pump and a repair kit, too. If it's pencils, they'll also need sharpeners.

◇ Consider asking the children's centre if you can sponsor a day out for the children while you're there. They generally get very little in the way of activities and experience, and a day at the beach, for example, will be remembered fondly for their entire lives. For your children, this will be a story and images that they will love. Our kids feel a strong allegiance to the children they left behind, and they like plenty of assurance that we've done and continue to do things to take care of them.

◇ Write your packing list and start to pack. Putting your new child's clothes into a bag is one of the most wonderful moments of adoption. Oh, the anticipation! Some suggestions for your travel bag:

    ◇ Something to read and watch yourself – remember, distraction is crucial for all the waiting around.

◊ Something to watch with your child, if they are slightly older. You will be exhausted by the level of energy your excited, eyes-opened-to-the-world child will have, especially if they are your first. On our first night together, one of our kids was fascinated with the lamp switch – she couldn't believe light would come on just from pushing it up. She turned it on and off and on and off and on and off and on and off. For hours.

◊ Spare copies of important documents.

◊ Appropriate clothes, at least some of which you look nice in – these will be your first photos with your child.

◊ A laptop or a journal to document some of your days – you will forget so much, so it's worth writing things down.

◊ Treats for your child and the other children. Pens, pencils, markers and paper are great to bring along for older kids, and allow you to do something together. A jigsaw is a good idea, too, as the other kids can get involved.

◊ Lots of hand sanitiser, band-aids, tissues, antiseptic cream and rehydration salts. Most of our older kids had skin issues and diarrhoea that were easily remedied with simple medical supplies.

◊ Vomit bags – kids who aren't used to travelling in cars and planes often struggle with motion sickness.

◊ Cutlery wrapped in a tea towel with a few plastic bags for impromptu meals.

◊ A special new toy for your child that you can keep for them. We took one of our girls a purple My Little Pony that got her past her initial shyness. We beaded its tail, brushed its hair and played with it for hours. She was concerned for the kids she was leaving behind, so she gave it to one of them, which makes me happy and sad at the same time.

◊ Other small things one of our older girls loved to play with at pick up was a little compact mirror, lipstick and stickers and plasters.

◇ If you're collecting a baby, remember a sling or kangaroo pouch. A buggy is pointless in most Third World countries, and the sling will really help with bonding in those first few weeks. We didn't use a buggy for the babies we adopted, even when they got home. They were permanently attached to us, and not only did this help with bonding, but also stopped strangers touching our already-traumatised infants.

◈ Start to prepare your friends and family for how you plan to parent your child when they first come home. We cover this in more detail later, but it is a very good idea to keep everyone away from the house for a while (perhaps two weeks), so the child starts to understand that whoever is in the house is their immediate family. At least for the first few months, you and your partner should perform the main caregiving activities (feeding, bathing, soothing, putting to sleep, etc.). This will help your child know that you are their parents and will be their main caregivers. Explain to your family that the child doesn't understand who their family is, and this early time is when they learn about their new situation. Tell your excited family and friends that you will visit them initially, and that you would prefer it if they didn't hold or feed the child (if a baby) or provide any other "parenting" services.

Why You Should Pick Up!

First things first, and this applies to international adoptions: please go and pick up your child. Really. I know that in some countries, where adoption is a well-oiled process, part of the arrangement includes someone dropping your child off with the birth country agents. Even if this option is available to you, don't take it.

There are two reasons why I recommend this so strongly. The first relates to your child's short-term adjustment, and the second to the long-term.

A baby or child being adopted has been through trauma already, no matter how young: the loss of their birth family and, in particular, their birth mother. No matter how great an adoptive mum I am, I cannot undo that wound. I can fill my child with so much love, but it will never, ever change the sadness she feels for her birth mother's loss.

Spending some time with your new child in their birth country, preferably in familiar surroundings, helps you start to create a bond, to start the journey from being a feared adult to becoming a friend and then a parent. I believe this will make the whole adoption transition process a little easier than starting in your home, never having spent time with them *in situ*. Your child will rarely have seen beyond the walls of the centre they live in. The overseas journey will be scary for them – a little less so, I think, with some time and preparation from you in their home country.

The second reason relates to their long-term adjustment. It makes such a difference to your child for you to be able to tell them what it was like in their birth country, what the food was like, and who used to look after them, as well as to show them photos. It also demonstrates to them a desire on your part to understand who they were before you. While it may never be said in so many words by the children, I think this is one of those very subtle things that will mean a lot.

I appreciate that some families struggle to fund adoptions, and that I am speaking from a position of privilege. But please think about what I have said here. OK, lecture over.

When you are finally given the go-ahead to travel to meet your child, it is one of the most magical, beautiful, euphoric feelings in the world.

What Pick-Up Is
Really Like

With our dossier submitted, all that was left was *the wait*. I was surprised by how painful this felt, and how drawn-out it seemed. Little did we know, this was the easy part.

In the months that followed, obsessively refreshing my email inbox became a ritual. Midnight, 3am, 6am – constantly! We received emails from the agency telling us to pray. *Pray?* I had never been religious and, up until that point, had lived in my own little world. During these months, however, I did pray, as I had nothing else. I was powerless, and had no control. The process began to change me. It wasn't just me, it was *us*! She was our daughter but she was faceless and ageless, and in the eyes of others, we were already becoming obsessive. A fictional person who may or may not be born was part of our family already – how was that possible?

One night, four months later, an email at last: "We have received a baby girl last night, she is severely malnourished, 6 months old and weighs less than 10lbs." No photo, no explanation, no background. I cried buckets that night, both happy and sad tears: devastation at the state of the little one, and excitement that she could be joining our family. We said yes: to what, exactly, we weren't sure. Now what? Now we get you the legal paperwork, they explained.

In the five months that followed, I lived on my computer. It was overwhelming, trying to hold down my job, stay strong and not appear like a raving lunatic, all the while aching to bring this child we had never met to the safety and security of "home".

Emails advised us to pray that she would survive the night as she was "in a bad state". *Might not survive the night?* What do you mean? She had IVs going into her skull, blood was taken from her neck, she was fed sugar sachets to keep her hydrated, and was patted with cold towels to keep her fever from rising too much with her weekly bouts of malaria. This felt like a horror film, and there was nothing we could do.

Finally, we got an email out the blue telling us she was legally ours and they would "be in touch in a month or two when her passport was ready". After trying to hold it together for months, I finally lost it. This tiny baby was legally ours, on the other side of the world, in desperate need of love, medical care and someone to cuddle – and I was being told to wait "a month or two" until I can take her out of the country.

My heart told me to resign from my job, say goodbye to friends, announce to the family why I had been a raving lunatic for a year, and board that plane. Within a week, we had packed a bag, booked seats on the weekly flight, and spent 23 hours flying to our destination, arriving in another world.

Damp, dusty, humid, we boarded the truck with no roof that collected us and went straight to the orphanage office. My brain was on repeat: "Where is my baby? Where is my baby?" I was taking care to appear somewhat normal to the staff, who insisted we take it easy, have a shower from the hosepipe, eat some rice and fish, and head to the children's centre in the morning.

Every minute of the next 16 hours felt even more tortured than the year that had passed. Just when you think you can't become any more of an emotional wreck, there's more waiting.

Finally, the next morning, the green van appeared – the transport to the orphanage, the medical facility, the driver's home, and our lifeline for the next six weeks. The drive was 20 minutes, but felt like days. When we walked in, they started by giving us a tour. A tour?! Anger swelled inside me: after all this time, *all this time*, I had zero interest in anything apart from our daughter. That sick little girl had been waiting nearly a year for me to scoop her up and cuddle her and never let go! *Someone find her!!*

Eventually, we walked into the baby room. I scanned my surroundings, about to self-combust at the thought that, after all these months, staring at photos and sleeping with my laptop, I may not be able to recognise her. What kind of mother would I be if I didn't recognise my child?! There was a sea of cots, crawling babies, sleeping toddlers, and an eerie silence, with the children not making any noise. Then my eyes fixed on this tiny bundle wedged between a nanny's legs, getting the tiniest tuft of hair braided. I desperately lifted the baby, *our* baby, up from her carer's knees. We cried and stared, stared and cried. She was limp, silent, so tiny and sick. At nearly 11 months old, she was still only 10lbs and not able to sit, make eye contact or even smile.

Within minutes, we were given a bottle and told that the van was waiting for us. That was it? No instructions, no clothes, no milk, no bottles, no nothing? Looking back, I feel naïve to have thought they were going to give me anything. But in that moment, I was shocked that they didn't lay out a schedule of feeding times for me, give me a bag of belongings, tell me her likes, dislikes.

Now onto the next twist: we were finally with our sick child, but with no way to go back home as we had no passport for her. Against the wishes of the orphanage, we'd travelled before it was ready, thinking that a month or two with us (even sleeping on the office floor) was better than without us. I honestly believe she would not be here today if we had not made this decision. She was so very, very sick.

The first thing we did was to remove her newborn vest and blue plastic bag nappy. She was clean and had been well looked after, but was so sad-looking. She didn't know how to laugh or interact. She stared silently into space, with no reaction or movement. Her legs were limp, and I turned to my husband and my mum: "Is something wrong with her spine?" I feared she couldn't use her legs – she could not sit unaided or bear any weight, despite being six weeks from her first birthday. All of a sudden, I was scared about what we might have taken on.

The next few weeks were hard – emotionally draining, mentally challenging, and such hard work. I've since given birth and, for me, the labour, breastfeeding, sleep deprivation, cracked nipples, leaking breasts, stitches and newborn issues were not a patch on this first six weeks with my adopted baby. She had never tasted solid food and was fed a few ounces of formula a day. I remember recording her progress in a tiny notepad and being so pleased when she took one ounce. Trying to feed her the rice cereals we'd brought with us was sad and distressing. I would put a blob on my little finger and lay it on her lip, and it just sat there. She just didn't know what to do with it.

Days turned into weeks, and we came to expect the unexpected. My husband returned home to work, as it was looking like we were here for the long haul. Mum continued to camp out with me. We befriended our security guards, who were so curious about our lives. "In your country, do you have dragons?" they asked. "When you are on the airplane, how do you know which stop to get off at?" They were mesmerised by our sachets of pot noodles and pureed potato transforming into full-blown meals within seconds of adding water.

Our baby all of a sudden started to flourish. She was helped by numerous green van visits to backstreet chemists to buy a single white pill to crush and give to her for her malaria, fever, septicaemia, scabies, conjunctivitis, chest infection, upper respiratory issues… the list went on. She began to amaze us daily. Within days, she was sitting (albeit limply) and starting to turn her head to sounds or movement. One night, I woke up startled (an otherworldly moment of "Do I actually have a baby"?) and as I flinched, I kicked her straight out of the bed onto the concrete office floor. Even despite this mother-of-the-year moment, she kept progressing.

It felt quite surreal after all of the waiting. Did someone actually allow me to mother this child? Is she really mine? Am I really here?

The excitement of making progress with her was offset by our frustration at not being able to get home. After six weeks of crisp sandwiches, powdered milk and pot noodles, we were so keen for a salad, a shower and our own homes. As my frustration started to bubble up again, I stormed into the Director's office and demanded he go straight to the Ministry of Foreign Affairs and find out where her passport was, or I was going to do… something. I can't remember what it was I said, but it would have been nonsensical as by then I was a crazy woman. Ironically, within 24 hours, we had a passport and a yellow fever vaccination certificate. The next flight out was days away, but that night we packed our hand luggage and gave everything we'd brought with us to the centre and staff, ready to leave with just a baby and a backpack!

The sweet relief of finally heading home! The airport was utter chaos. People, smells, queues, bags. We had gone to the airline office in town to buy the infant ticket we needed and confirm our adult tickets. It was all easy, and we were given printed tickets.

Arriving at the check-in desk a few hours later, it was comforting to recognise the same lady who had printed out our tickets was also going to check us in. But when we handed over our paperwork, she calmly stated that we didn't have tickets. Um, yes, we do, you printed these a few hours ago. "You need to buy another ticket," she told us. "Why?" we asked. We argued for over 30 minutes while my daughter lay limply against me, sweating in a sling. "You people need to buy more tickets," she kept insisting. We quickly realised that if we wanted to get on the *only* plane that week, we would need to cough up. "How much?" we asked her. "$1200 each." *Seriously?* We started pulling cash out of our bum bags and handed it over; we were absolutely desperate to leave.

I was crying my eyes out, in between almost laughing hysterically at the situation. We eventually got through security and waited for a plane that would leave "when everyone gets here".

Finally, we arrived in the country where we would take our connecting flight to Dubai. We were late and had missed our connection (in all subsequent trips, we have not once made this connection). It was pitch black, very late, and the arrivals area was a sea of taxi touters. We chose one and asked the driver to take us to any airport hotel.

Two hours later, sitting in the taxi down a dark alley and feeling utterly petrified, I phoned home to Dubai. The driver had been jumping out at every hotel, only to return with the news that they were full. After the fifth or sixth time this happened, I began to get suspicious. I was freaking out to my husband on the phone, and he was thousands of miles away, powerless to help. Having spent days in immigration and every official office in Dubai, trying to get an entry visa for a child with a different surname with documents that weren't attested by anyone of remote significance, he was ready to snap, too. He screamed at me to put the driver on the phone; I worried that might aggravate the situation further and see the driver take us down one last dark alley and dispose of us completely.

Instead, I started pretending I was scared of my boss man, and that boss man was telling me to hurry up and get to the hotel or he would call the police. Lo and behold, within five minutes we were dropped off at a high-rise dive for the night. I've never been so grateful to see a lockable room, despite the TV with no wires, a lamp with no bulb, an air conditioning unit full of rodents, and a solitary towel that was used as soon as we got there to wipe the yellow diarrhoea from my baby, as she lay limp and dehydrated. We celebrated our last night before home with what we could get: a vodka and Fanta, and a bowl of fries.

The final blow to my sanity came the next morning, as we boarded the airport bus. An American man asked how much my daughter had cost me. At this early stage, I was still naïve in my handling of this line of questioning; I stuttered and said pardon. He repeated his question, and added, "I hear these things are expensive these days." I got off the bus and recognised that this was the start of a lifetime of ridiculously rude, ignorant and plain stupid questions.

We were utterly exhausted when we arrived back in Dubai – mentally drained, and emotionally a wreck. My husband was waiting at the airport for us. I was so grateful to be able to hand over the baby and know that she would be safe: the responsibility that I had shouldered for the last six weeks could be shared now with someone else.

Being home was surreal – it was hard to comprehend the experience we'd just had, and the long, emotional rollercoaster that had come before it. At last, I was starting to relax and enjoy our new family.

◆ ◆ ◆

Tips to survive pick-up:

◈ I can promise you that pick-up will, for the most part, not live up to the romantic experience you imagine. There *will* be parts that are life-altering and amazing, but they will be interspersed with much frustration. All of the strategies I recommend for the wait, I recommend for pick-up, too. In these days of iPads and downloadable Netflix, take a device full of programmes for you as well as some that are appropriate for the age of your child. There will be lots of waiting around, and you will *still* need to distract yourself. You're nearly there.

◈ Focus your mind and heart on the moment you see your child for the first time. Do not video it. This is for your family, not the world. Take plenty of footage later, but the moment you meet them, you want them seeing *you*, not an iPhone. The moments we met each of our kids are burned into our brains – we don't need videos to remind us.

◈ Do not for a second worry about spoiling your newly adopted child. Give them a million cuddles, buckets of affection, stroke them and brush their hair and feed them and do whatever makes them happy.

◈ Collect stories from and photos of the people who loved your child before the adoption – they will ask for these later, and it will help connect them to their early days. Our kids love us telling them who they played with, which big kids loved them the most, what their nicknames were, whether they cried a lot, what they liked to do, etc.

◈ Take photos of where they slept and played, as well as the centre and its surroundings, to show them later. I certainly felt weird taking a picture of the bed, but I knew I'd be pleased that I did down the track (and I have been).

◈ If you can, take an item of clothing that they wore at the centre, and put it in a Ziploc bag. Don't wash it. A smell can remind you of so much – the scent of the soap, and the clothes themselves, can be powerful connectors when your child is in need of them.

◈ I brought home local newspapers, a piece of wood from the beach, some local currency, a hotel leaflet, a few business cards of people we met, and some receipts of things we bought. All of this is kept in little Ziploc bags in memory boxes, and everything has a story.

◈ You are unlikely to get much detail from the centre, but an understanding of your child's likes, routines and habits would obviously be helpful.

◈ While sightseeing is the last thing you will feel like doing, try to take a few hours here and there to see a bit of your child's country. The kids do ask to see these photos from time to time.

◈ If you're spending time at the children's centre, the other kids are likely to want some attention and affection from you. It's helpful to take things for the kids left behind, like soccer balls with a pump and repair kit, drawing pads and pencils with a sharpener, clothes, treats, etc. The centre will tell you what the necessities are, but some fun stuff will also be greatly appreciated by the kids.

◈ When it comes to travel, we've found our adopted kids are very extreme in their behaviour. Some of them sit quietly on a flight or in a car, and won't eat or use the bathroom for hours on end. One of our kids sat through a 15-hour flight without food or using the toilet, and only begrudgingly took a sip of water at our insistence. This child suffers from motion sickness even on a plane, so we carry Kwells and a vomit bag, and otherwise let her sleep for as long as she wants to. When she does get off the plane, she will be ravenous and need to eat immediately. It can be frustrating when she's declined all offers of plane food, so we always have a few food options ready in our bag. Other children are hyperactive from start to finish, and need a new activity or to kick the seat in front (sorry!) every five minutes. Take activities and snacks, so that you're prepared to cater for both extremes.

◊ In the early days of travelling with the kids, I'd pack a Ziploc bag full of Cheerios and lengths of wool or leather. The kids would thread the loops on to make a necklace, I'd tie it on and they'd bite the loops off happily. Even my most active traveller loved this activity. In fact, I need to bring this back for my younger kids!

◊ If you are picking up a walking child, try to tire them out with physical movement before you board the plane. A swim is great, and even walking laps at the airport will work.

Sleepless Early Days

When my baby finally came home, I was relieved and excited. I was ready to relax into our new routine together. She was the most angelic child in the daytime – she rarely cried, didn't move much and was just like an extension of me wherever I went. I thought I had this exceptionally good child, but looking back a decade later, I realise how much she was hurting, how painful it was for her, even as a baby.

Despite her behaviour in the daytime, she was having none of my plans for relaxing into our new family after dark. She took at least two hours to get to sleep at night. She gave up daytime naps shortly after her first birthday, but despite being even more tired, she was still impossible to settle at night. We rocked her in a car seat on her bedroom floor, paced the corridor, patted her back, co-slept, slept in total darkness, left the light on, put her down in cots, beds, sofas, prams… the child just *did not sleep*. She would wake up ten to twelve times a night, for no apparent reason.

Little did we know this was the start of three years of nocturnal madness. Every night, we'd be woken repeatedly by a little hand tapping on our shoulders: "My eye hurts. My leg is itchy. I need water. I want a wee. There are monsters".

A typical night would see me up for hours trying to settle her. I would put her to bed and attempt to commando-crawl across the floor to exit without her seeing me. She caught me, always. After the fifth or sixth round of this, occasionally I'd storm out, burst into tears and pace the corridor for probably 30 seconds, chanting: "She's only a baby, she's only a baby." I'd regain my composure and enter for the next round. It was endless.

I have a vivid memory of one night when she was probably two and a half and I was heavily pregnant. I had a mini-meltdown (these were becoming more frequent) and told my husband I could no longer deal with her while this pregnant or, in a few weeks, nursing a newborn. On this particular night, I declared that he was in charge. By 2am, he was sitting on a desk chair in the middle of the landing outside her bedroom, asleep, with a pair of boxer shorts on and the floor rug draped over him (I have no idea why he didn't take a blanket from another bedroom). Every time she got up and tried to escape past him, he flinched, told her to get back to bed, and then drifted back to sleep himself. He estimated that she was up 14 times that night, and admittedly, he became super-dad through the night after that.

◆ ◆ ◆

Everyone says that sleep deprivation is a form of torture. I'd heard that a million times, but I didn't *really* understand until my sleep deprivation was so extreme that I went crazy!

When we brought our baby home, I loved waking to him in the night, rocking and feeding him. I didn't mind that he often didn't respond to my efforts – I understood that this was all new, that all this love and attention was confusing to him. For two months, I carried on, falling further and further in love with our little boy, devoted and patient.

Then, all of a sudden, the honeymoon was over. *So* over. I was so tired I thought I was dying. There was no pattern to his sleep, and therefore no pattern to mine. One hour, three hours, half an hour, one hour. All night. Every night. I would be delighted to get three or four hours in a row. But it was never, ever more than that. Most of the time, one hour of sleep at a time was as good as I would get.

I had endured interrupted sleep before – I had two biological girls who breastfed at night until they were almost two. I thought I knew tired. I thought I could handle tired.

Ha. I didn't know what tired was. *Nobody* knew what tired was. This was a whole new experience. And it sent me mad.

Rather than finishing each day looking forward to relaxing in the evening, darkness would bring on this fretful anxiety. Do I go to sleep as soon as he does, so I get some more sleep? Or do I spend a couple of hours as a sane adult, enjoying adult company and relaxing without a psycho toddler around? I was so torn: sleep, or peace? If I slept, it wouldn't be for long and it would mean I'd have no time to myself all day. If I stayed up, I would get some me time, but when he woke up ten minutes after I'd fallen asleep, I would kick myself. What to do, what to do?

Either way, I didn't get enough sleep and I didn't get enough peace. I staggered through life, somehow still managing to enjoy some of it. I didn't quite enjoy my little boy, though. Both of us were a mess at night, and therefore a mess during the day. I had little or no patience with him, and he had little or no tolerance for things that didn't go his way. His often strange behaviour was starting to really grate on me, and his need for my attention every minute was taking its toll.

My toddler would wake up and I would creep into his room, feeling as kind and selfless as Mother Teresa. I would spend ten minutes being calm and focused, speaking gently and kindly. When he didn't respond, I would rock him, rub his back, sing. When he screamed and kicked me, when he hit me and hissed at me, I would try to recall all I had read in my adoption books, my self-help books, my calming meditation books. *Help me, books. Help me now!* Forget it. The wisdom was gone. My voice would get louder, my tone more and more unhinged, and the anger and tiredness were back.

For three and a half years – that's about 15,650 days – this continued nightly. I went to see psychologists for advice on how to deal with it. Two changed my mindset and started to put me back on the path to sanity again. The first asked me a barrage of questions before declaring: "You are not the one who is crazy and needs to change. He is."

This I knew, but how could I expect this small child to change?

The psychologist told me we had done the work that meant he *was* attached and bonded. He simply needed to learn to sleep. My husband had been suggesting for many nights in that three-and-a-half-year period that I try not going in to him at night. He assured me he would be fine. But I was so worried – this poor baby, he needed to know he had a mother who would come when he needed her. Well, three and a half years later, he certainly knew that I would come.

The psychologist talked me through everything. He convinced me that my child was now securely attached, and that the most important thing at that time was for both of us to get some sleep. I trusted him. I was finally ready to believe that that was the truth. So my mind was made up: I was going to put him to bed that night, tell him it was time for sleep, and kiss him and hug him like I always did. But this time, when he woke up and called out, I would only go and check on him once. If he was safe and not ill, then I would tell him I was going to sleep because it was night-time and I would see him when we both woke up in the morning. I had my plan. I was all set. I was preparing for weeks of listening to him crying and screaming and me feeling awful and ending up just going in and him hitting me and screaming some more.

I put him to bed that night, I kissed and hugged him and told him it was time for sleep. At that moment, he stared at me. He stared deeply into my eyes for what felt like an eternity. I said goodnight and walked out of the room. He slept soundly through the night, and didn't wake up during the night again.

Incredible. This intuitive, clever little boy knew that my mind had been changed, that I was now ready to let go and get some sleep. He saw it in my eyes. He somehow felt my energy had shifted and decided that he, too, was ready.

I am certain that had I tried to do it before then, it may not have worked. I had to reach the point where I knew that sleep was more important than anything else. My absolute determination to ensure that my child knew I was his mother, that I would care for him and love him and attend to his every need, outweighed my need for sleep. It wasn't until I realised I couldn't carry on like that anymore, that I was in fact being a lesser mother because I felt so tired, that I was ready to let go.

A couple of years later, another psychologist spoke to me about this time in our lives. She asked me what I would do when I went in to him at night. I answered that I would rub his back, tell him he was safe and loved, ask him what he needed, hug him. She then asked what he did. Well, he thrashed around in bed, kicking, screaming, grunting when I asked what was wrong... She asked me what I thought was wrong with him. I didn't know. I knew he was confused. That he wanted love and affection, but didn't quite know how to deal with it. She asked me if I ever told him it was OK to be angry, scared and confused. She said it would have been nice if I'd told him he was safe to thrash and kick and let it all out; if I'd told him I understood that he was angry and felt out of control.

I cried. I hadn't done this. I had tried to make it better. I had tried to fix him myself. And I had felt so frustrated and angry that he wasn't responding to my efforts. But all he needed was to feel supported and safe to let it all out. He needed me to *let him be*. To let him express his feelings of anger and confusion and frustration. To let him thrash and scream without someone trying to stop him. Without someone trying to rock it out of him, to make him a nice, quiet baby who slept.

If I'd had this advice earlier, I think he would have expressed himself openly and probably stopped the waking, thrashing and screaming earlier on. He would have felt understood and supported, instead of feeling bad for not responding to the mother who was so desperately trying to fix him. And I would have gotten about 125,000 more hours of sleep.

◆ ◆ ◆

While we certainly have some sleep horror stories, some of our kids have always gone to bed happily, stayed in their beds without incident, and woken at a decent hour, refreshed and ready for a new day. One of the girls was so used to being in a cot all day and night as a toddler in the centre that she slept for 16 hours solid, without a peep, when she came home. Even when she did eventually wake at 10am, she would just sit there in her bed, in silence, until someone came and got her.

One of our boys would play hard all day and, when he was a toddler, he regularly fell asleep in his dinner. Always a hungry boy, he'd never (never!) agree to go to bed when there was uneaten food in front of him, and he'd have closed eyes while still chewing. If we attempted to move him and get him back to bed, he'd wake up and protest. Once in bed, though, he'd sleep well.

His sleep issues came later on. Once he'd been with us a few years, we noticed his eyes were regularly bloodshot. When we saw this, we'd also observe the edgy, agitated behaviour of an overtired child the same day. His teacher started to call to say he was falling asleep in class. We tried putting him to bed even earlier, but it didn't improve things at all.

Then we started to hear noises in the night, and the penny dropped. He was going to bed, sleeping a while and then getting up in the middle of the night. He'd have a midnight snack, "quietly" play with some toys, or wander the hallway. He was far less attached than some of the other kids, and he'd not once tried to jump into bed with us. (In fact, he has never tried to climb into bed with us). We'd hear him and get up and patiently (or grumpily, depending on the situation) put him back to bed. Usually, we'd hear him singing and playing in his bed, sometimes for hours. We'd leave him to it as long as he wasn't waking up the others, but grow increasingly annoyed and then not be able to sleep ourselves.

This sleep pattern lasted a long time, and we tried everything to break it: star charts for sleeping in his bed all night, rewards, punishments, changes to night-time routines – we searched for years and years for a solution. We eventually took him to the doctor and she referred us to a psychiatrist, who suggested we medicate him in order for him to get some sleep. This was not our first medication rodeo, and while we had started out vehemently opposed to medicating children, we now knew it could help them get through rough patches and save not only their sanity, but ours, too. So he started taking medication to boost his melatonin, and all of a sudden, our boy could stay asleep through the night. It was revolutionary for him, and for us. He stayed on this medication for some months until we, and he, felt he didn't need it anymore. Most nights now he sleeps with no issues at all.

◆   ◆   ◆

Some tips for sleep-challenged kids (and parents) that start out fairly stock-standard and then get a little more unusual:

◊ Try to stick to a regular sleep routine:

  ◊ No screens right before bed.

  ◊ No sugar after dinner.

  ◊ Restricted water after dinner.

  ◊ Reading a bedtime story.

  ◊ Singing a lullaby.

  ◊ Lots of exercise during the day – you want them falling into bed!

  ◊ If they have no health issues, load them up on carbohydrates for dinner. In addition to being a favourite food of kids, it should help lull them to sleep.

◊ Try massage to calm your child. Before you feel distressed at the thought of adding "massage therapist" to your already-long list of roles, and oil and a massage table to your already-long list of things to buy, stop: this is not how we roll.

  We have two quick, effective and equipment-free approaches. The first is massaging the ears, from the cartilage at the top down to the lobe, pulling the ear gently out from the head and rubbing it between your fingers, and rolling it back and then forwards.[4] My kids melt at this instant stress-reducer. I also use it if they are really upset, or if they are struggling with cabin pressure on planes. I do it to myself to calm down or when I feel a cold coming on. I'm always surprised how stressed and lumpy my ears feel when I start on them. This is actually called "thinking caps" in the world of kinesiology and brain gym, and we've since been told by professionals that it's an actual technique to ease anxiety.

---

4 www.lionheartfamilies.com/resources

The second technique goes like this: when the kids are laying in bed with their covers pulled up, stand over them and, with an open hand, press down on their body, walking your hands from the top of the back to the lower back, bum, and legs, and spending lots of time on the feet. Turn them over and do the same to the front of the legs and top of the feet. You can do it while singing a lullaby to them. Watch your child turn to putty in your hands.[5]

If you see an Occupational Therapist for a child with sensory processing issues, they will often recommend body brushing. We did this for a while with a couple of our guys, and it worked well. In our experience, the pressing described above works just as well without the need for equipment.

◈   Here's one you'll find curious: wrestling before bed is an almost daily occurrence in our home. After teeth are brushed and our boy is ready for bed, he and his dad will stand in the hallway, lock shoulders and try to push the other over some imaginary line. There's a lot of grunting, sledging, laughing and collapsing. He adores it, both at a physical level and as a way to connect with his dad. He'll ask for it if it's not offered. Some parents might discount this, as I originally did, out of concern that it would hype him up right before bed. But we have been using this strategy for probably a year, and the impact is quite the opposite. It helps him calmly get to sleep, whereas he used to be very twitchy and up-and-down to the point where we'd eventually shout at him to go to sleep. Wrestling is tactile, playful and great relational interaction for a child: one-on-one, turn-taking, with lots of pressure, pushing and gently playing, teaching your child how to use their energy and then control it in a fun way. For children who crave sensory input, the wrestling and squeezing calms their central nervous system and helps them to be ready to rest when they get into bed, instead of bouncing on the bed or fiddling with toys for hours.

◈   Sensory pressure while sleeping helps some kids tremendously. Some of our kids love sleeping with a weighted blanket on them.

---

5 www.lionheartfamilies.com/resources

It provides enough pressure and associated sensory feedback that the kids are calmed immensely. You can buy these online from occupational therapy stores.

◊ Consider leaving a light on. Remember that your child is likely to have had lots of people around and may find your quiet house and their quiet room frightening. One of our kids has slept with a light on since she came home, and we used to wonder how she got any sleep. But she does.

◊ None of us consciously or deliberately co-slept with our kids in the early days. We would let them crawl into bed with us or bring them in on the odd occasion, but it was never a planned strategy. Now, we would say that for kids who are traumatised and afraid, whether initially or down the track, try co-sleeping until they are calmer, even if they are older. They get comfort, security, increased bonding with you and the entire family gets more sleep.

◊ Co-sleeping is *not* just for babies. We don't worry about creating bad habits in older kids; they will tell you when they don't want to co-sleep anymore. I've co-slept with an older child for the last nine months, as she's been having quite a hard time processing all that's happened in her life. We are closer than we have ever been, and she has felt safe, secure and loved. It's about the right time for her to return to her room now, but I'll probably have her stay with me one night at the weekend so we can watch shows together, I can hug her, and we can talk. Don't forget, co-sleeping is parenting while lying down, and that, in our books, is a winning parenting approach.

High-Vis Parenting

In the early years of our adoptive parenting journey, I felt on show. It seemed to me that any misstep I made in parenting would be critiqued by a world keen to give feedback to flailing new parents, particularly new parents with obviously adopted children.

We have each of us had some memorable public parenting moments.

An early one was bringing home my daughter for the first time, alone. She was happy to spend time with me peacefully, but when it came to waiting around in an airport for hours for a delayed flight, she became a headcase. I had a bag full of snacks, colouring-in books, pencils and stickers (sadly, it was before the iPad came around, so my arsenal was all analogue). We would start an activity – say, make a few strokes on the page with a pencil – and within a minute she'd start rifling through the bag for something else. She ate the entire stash of snacks that were intended to sustain us through the long flight, and then proceeded to vomit all over herself, me and the airport floor.

You may wonder why I was such a pushover, giving in to her every demand. Well, I was alone, taking an adopted child out of her birth country. I was self-conscious and wanted to get home without any trouble. Just a few weeks before, a friend of a friend had ended up under house arrest through some misunderstanding with the police. So yes, I was going along with my girl to try and fly under the radar a bit and keep the peace, at least until we got home, where I would "start parenting".

Some women helped me clean her up and while they had questions, they were not judgemental. I think I had some romantic notion that I was parenting children of the world, and that other adults might have a higher benchmark because we had chosen to parent children born to other parents.

Another public parenting moment we remember was a regular occurrence for a while. Most weekends, we took our family to a café for breakfast. If our adopted child saw an adult of his racial background, he would catapult himself out of his highchair and throw himself at them. The adult, mid-coffee order or mid-bite, would look at us wide-eyed, stunned and not sure how to react. We would mumble a hurried explanation – I can't really remember what. ("Sorry! He thinks you're his mother/father…?!") It made me feel silly, like a parental imposter, and so very, very white.

Another of us had this misdirected need to project perfect, Mary Poppins-worthy parenting skills on first bringing a new child home to add to her family of two other children. She was determined to ensure her eldest child's first days of school were a success, despite the arrival of the newly adopted child and a new baby. She'd walk exactly seven minutes down the road to and from school each day to drop off her girl, and return in the afternoon to pick her up. She knows it was seven minutes, because she had timed the horror. She would walk along, smiling, hoping no one would notice her adopted child screaming and angrily kicking at the baby lying above her in a double buggy. On every single trip, she would have to stop and rescue the baby and put him in the carrier.

Once at school, her adopted child would instantly stop screaming and kicking, and would smile and chat with the security guard. She'd then turn her back to her mother and start screaming again. All the while, mum would simply grip her hand and not respond to any of this behaviour, while kissing the schoolgirl goodbye and wishing her a good day. She would pretend she could neither see nor hear the feral one. Everyone she walked past looked a bit confused by the spectacle.

These few examples came to us in seconds; there are many more where they came from. We share these examples for two reasons.

The first is that, as a new adoptive parent, you may feel that you need to be better, calmer and more patient than the next parent, because you are parenting children not biologically yours. You signed up and went through training and counselling, plus the kids have had a hard start to life. Then, as you get into adoptive parenting, you may feel frustrated with yourself as you fail to live up to your own expectations and your sense of what society expects of you. After a decade of parenting, we've realised that no one is really paying that much attention, and no one (except perhaps *you*) are expecting better parenting than average. So let that one go.

The second reason that we share these memories is that your adopted children, with their attachment and trauma issues, are reasonably likely to act up in public. It can be hard to parent the way your child needs you to when you feel that others around you consider your approach harsh. We've all had occasions where we've disciplined our kids in the way we believe is appropriate, only to have family or friends pipe up to tell us they're "just kids", or that we need to relax a bit. No one who has parented an adopted child has ever, ever said that to us. You need to parent consistently, inside the home and out of it, to make your children feel safe, to ensure they don't get confused, and so that you don't end up confused yourself.

If you feel pressure to be better, to be more, because you are parenting adopted children, we strongly suggest you get over it. If you feel pressured to change what your instincts or your research tells you are the right parenting methods for your adopted child because those around you think your parenting is uncaring or extreme or spectacularly unsuccessful, we strongly suggest you get over it. Please do not seek parenting approval from the world at large, because the world at large has very little insight into what you deal with day to day.

Years of experience have allowed us to feel less concerned about what people think of our parenting. Even now, our patience is often stretched, meaning we're prone to losing it spectacularly now and again. On a recent overseas holiday, for example, my girl asked to do some shopping, so we spent an hour at H&M looking for things for her. I was her lackey: I carried the clothes she'd selected to try on, changed sizes, and ferried things back and forth. After an hour, she chose only a couple of things, I paid and we left. To this day, she assures me she said thank you, but it was not loud or grateful enough to satisfy me. I let her know in no uncertain terms how ungrateful she was being. She just shrugged a little and demanded to go.

That tipped me over the edge, and I could no longer control my anger. I grabbed the yellow shopping bag off her and swung it around and around in circles, like some kind of helicopter, before launching it onto the concrete in front of the shop. Then I turned on my heel and walked off. I could feel the eyes of the families sitting around the fountain watching me. Some time ago, I would have cared; now I don't. I stormed off in a huff, and then realised she didn't know how to get back to the hotel. So I hid around the corner, where I waited for her. She didn't quite smile when she saw me, but looked slightly bemused.

Here are some tips that are perhaps stating the obvious when it comes to surviving high-vis parenting:

◈ The most important advice we have is to care less about what people think of you and your parenting. Let it go! Just like you say to your teenage children: everyone is actually too busy thinking about what everyone else thinks about *them*, to think about you. We no longer over-explain, or even try to explain at all.

◈ When your patience is worn thin, or your child is struggling, try to be gentler in your expectations. Do you *really* need to go to the post office today? Can you divide and conquer with your partner or a family member? If you really must do something, chat with your kids honestly about how everyone is feeling, and ask for their help in cooperating with you. The pep talk rarely delivers the desired results, but it will help moderate behaviour as you don't need to have it in public – you simply need to remind the kids of what you talked about.

◈ If you are using therapeutic parenting, or dealing with some behavioural issues you need to work on with your child regularly, communicate this to the people you closely interact with – like family, friends, and their school teacher. Acknowledge that your parenting methods may seem hard, but explain that you believe they are necessary and you'd like their support.

◊ Be patient if your child acts up in public. Try to take them to a quiet spot and sit with them for a bit until they calm down. Don't get stressed if you need to take more severe action and, say, end your child's after-school activity early because of their bad behaviour (we have each of us taken extreme measures with our kids when their behaviour was really out of order). There is no shame in going home.

Oh, the Questions
You'll Be Asked!

I remember my first coffee morning with my adopted child, meeting a friend who had also just had a baby. By coincidence, another of her friends joined us with her baby son. As soon as I introduced myself, things started unravelling. She immediately gave me the "Oh, so sad" look as she stroked my girl's arm and asked me how many times I'd had IVF before I had to adopt her.

I was taken aback by such a personal question, and started to stutter as she finished off with, "Oh, and a black child, too – bless you." I quickly moved from stunned to angry, and it boiled over quickly. I spat back, "How many times did you have sex before you conceived him?" She was visibly appalled. I turned to my friend and said I didn't want to spend time with someone so rude – sorry, I had to go. My heart was pounding. Thankfully, the baby was oblivious to the whole scenario.

This shocker of an experience was the start of learning how to build a protective shield around our family. As I've become more experienced, my responses are less volatile, while remaining firm in terms of protecting my family. We also teach the kids that sometimes, people can be busybodies, naïve, uneducated, or simply rude.

The combination of our family growing and its composition being hard to figure out means we do get plenty of double takes when we are out in public. However, our experience in learning to avoid questions and over-the-top attention means that few people approach us.

As well as getting less attention over time, I'm pleased the kids are learning to deflect the questions gracefully. If someone asks, "Is she your real mum?", they might laugh and say, "Well, she's not plastic". When I hear this sarcasm, I figure we're doing something right – making these discussions taboo or heated is not going to get them anywhere.

Even our biological child rolls his eyes when someone comments about his mum being white and his sisters being black. He answers, "Duh, that's cos my sisters are from Africa." I had to correct him, though, when he started telling people he didn't have a birth mother and he was adopted from Scotland. I was forced to get out the photos to convince him I was indeed his birth mother!

I encourage others, as they look at a family that is different to theirs: think, people, think. Every question you ask is heard by little ears. Now, if I see a family that is interesting – whether it's multiple kids, mixed race, or otherwise hard to figure out – I would sooner poke myself in the eye than intrude on that family with a question that really doesn't matter to me, and that they have probably deflected a million times already.

◆ ◆ ◆

I looked at my two little ones with pride (at the time, I wasn't to know that their school uniforms would never be so spotless again!). Their hair was perfect, their faces were clean, and they looked so grown up. My heart ached at the realisation of how much time had passed since I'd become their mother. This wistfulness, for me, has always been amplified by having missed some of their start to life. We dropped them off at school, two obviously white parents with two obviously non-white children.

In a new situation, the tricky dance starts – the dance of how to present my family honestly and proudly, while gracefully fobbing off intrusive questions, without offending the mother of my child's new friend, or their new teacher.

I found this dance absolutely excruciating at the start. My husband was blunt and verged on being rude, and was textbook in his responses. I kept getting tripped up by my natural openness and my desire to make friends, for both me and my children. Many a day I would come home from an outing, replaying a conversation in my head, annoyed by how much I'd spoken about the kids. It felt like I was betraying them, but I found it extremely hard to deal with the friendly interrogations.

Deflecting questions from strangers is far easier than handling questions from people you kind-of know or might want to know. When your family is new to a school, a class or a group, its par for the course to undergo some interrogation. Originally, we found this hard: you want your child to fit in, to make friends, and you don't want to get a reputation as precious.

It starts with, *Oh, you're Freddy's mum, he's so cute, where's he from?* You answer that question simply, and the rest unfolds the same way pretty much every time.

Do you have any other children?

Are they adopted too?

Oh wow, are they siblings?

Are their parents dead?

All with your child there. Yep. Pretty much guaranteed.

Oh, the awkwardness I have felt! The class mum coffee mornings, where our family becomes a very interesting topic. The mums who've watched us drop off and pick up and have been just dying to ask. I get it: if I weren't in the firing line myself, I'd probably be curious, too. And certainly, when I see a family at school I find fascinating, I too will wonder – is that her dad or her husband? Are all those kids theirs? Is it a second marriage? But while I might wonder what their story is, my questions do not leave the confines of my brain. Because the reality is, the answers to these questions matter little to me, beyond satisfying my curiosity. They don't change my day, let alone my life – unless, of course, we become friends with that family, and then they'll tell me what they want to tell me in their own time.

So here's how to deal with this series of questions: tell the truth, up to the sibling question. Then, my strong advice, learned through years of trial and error, is that no matter what the biological truth may be, say *yes*, they are siblings. Often, people will clarify: "I mean birth siblings?" Just say yes. It's nobody's business, and as an adoptive family you've already concluded that the creation of a family isn't reliant on biological ties. To answer any other way – and I have done so many, many times – is to invite a whole other line of deeply personal questions that are even harder to squirm out of.

The other thing is, no one *really* cares that much, unless they are close to you, in which case they'll know the truth. This little white lie protects some boundaries for your kids, cuts off a potentially volatile line of questioning, and satisfies someone who's not actually that bothered either way.

Within our tribe, we have some kids that are very close in age. This gives rise to another very predictable grouping of questions:

Oh wow, they are in the same grade? Are they twins?

(Um, no. One was adopted, one is biological. Or no, they were adopted. Cue a new set of tricky questions.)

Again, all with your child or children there. Yep. Pretty much guaranteed.

As people come to understand that they are most certainly not twins, and that one or both were adopted, they'll comment something like, "Ohhhh, so not real sisters then?" Our standard response to this is, "Yes, they are sisters, but they are from different countries." I don't think there is an easy way out of this one. Just be prepared with a family-specific answer, with the main message being that family comes first and they are, without question, brothers and sisters.

Instead of agonising over what to say, set a boundary in your head for the couple of questions you're happy to answer. For anything beyond that, simply say, "It's complicated." I've rarely had someone come back for a second round after that answer. If they do keep going, I tend to say something like, "I'm happy to tell my story, but this is my child's, and not mine, to tell." It's friendly but clear, and respectful of my kids.

◆ ◆ ◆

Tips for dealing with awkward questions:

◊ First and foremost, remember that most people really aren't interested in your answers. They are simply curious, and don't realise how intrusive and laced with emotion their questions are.

◊ Even if you are normally open and honest, accept that you won't always be able to behave normally when you are trying to create and maintain some boundaries for your family. Being protective of your children, in our view, should outweigh your own desire to be truthful to a fault.

◊ Don't throw the ball up: don't make eye contact or smile at curious onlookers, and don't say things that invite further questions.

◊ Stay calm and don't get weird when you start getting the questions. This is harder than it sounds: you *will* feel weird and awkward. Once you've set your mental boundary, it is a lot easier to relax.

◊ Have your go-to phrase ready when you don't want to keep answering questions. Mine is, "It's complicated." Others use "It's private", "That's not my story to tell", "That's personal" or even a question back: "Why do you ask?" The sarcastic "Pardon?" often works a treat, too.

Accept that sometimes, you will need to unwind a harmless lie. For example, when someone asks some questions that go beyond your boundaries, and you need to fob them off. Later on, they may become family friends and it's appropriate that they understand the scenario a little better. I've found that being honest in explaining why you tend to avoid the questions is easily understood.

You Can't Put a Genie Back in the Bottle: Telling Your Story

As your child gets older, talk to them about what they feel comfortable disclosing. I feel that there is not one thing in my son's past that he should feel ashamed of. I tell him repeatedly that he should be proud of his story and his journey.

As your children get older, they may feel fine about answering questions from adults directly. I am a naturally open person who finds it very difficult not to answer people's questions – especially when they are coming from a good-natured place. While I am getting better at coming up with a quick reply to put rude people in their place, when it comes to answering questions about my son, I feel that it is his story to tell, so I don't want to disclose things without his permission. As he is growing, so is his confidence. He has been happily telling people that he went to meet his birth family recently. I give him free reign in this department, and I'm happy that he is proud and confident enough to do so.

◆ ◆ ◆

It's been a surprise to us how old the kids are before they start getting quizzed about their families by other kids at school. It takes years for the kids to register that their family is different, and to wonder why. The longer you have been part of a community, the more this is true – often, it's the new activities, new schools, or new towns that unearth this type of questioning.

Our kids each know as much as we do about their family backgrounds. We are open and honest, and don't sugar-coat things (even though sometimes all we want to do is sugar-coat things).

Young kids are straightforward little souls. Kids have asked our adopted kids every conceivable question:

"Is your real mum dead?"

"Why didn't your real mum want you?"

"Why couldn't your mum have babies herself?"

"Did your mum buy you?"

These are tough questions and horrible sentiments that are asked innocently, but if your child isn't prepared for them, they could really hurt.

You need to start arming your children with responses to questions from other kids as young as possible, and change them as your child grows. Teach them statements like:

◈ My birth mother couldn't look after me.

◈ Those questions are very personal to me.

◈ My mum is real, touch her.

◈ I was born in...

◈ I was adopted when I was two years old.

A good strategy for both adults and children feeling as though they're being interrogated is to turn questions back to the other person. *Tell me about your family? Where were you born? Why do you want to know that?*

You need to keep reiterating to your child that it is up to them who they share their story with. It's essential to keep reminding them that there is nothing to be ashamed of, that while their story might be different, it is their special story. We do speak to the kids about taking care with who they trust with this information as once told, a story can't be untold. It can be hard for kids, who trade information like currency, to withhold something, but it's a skill they need to develop for their own peace of mind.

Have this conversation with your child at the start of every school year, when taking on new activities, and when they have a new teacher or friend.

Shattering the Mother Teresa Myth

It started in their birth country. We were at the airport with two children, armed with drink bottles and colouring books, attempting to explain to them what would happen next. These were children who could count the number of car rides they'd had on one hand, nevermind the helicopter airport transfer they'd just enjoyed, and the 747 they were about to board for the flight "home".

Passport control. We travelled a lot in the early days and, over time, became accustomed to the circus it involved: passports, visas, adoption documents ("Do you have the originals?"), spot checks on our story to convince themselves that the children were ours ("Is this your mummy? What is her name?"). This first time, though, the officials were beaming beautiful smiles and wishing us well. "You are good Christians," they said. "These children are so lucky. You are so, so good. May God bless you."

And so it began.

The Mother Teresa analogy very often follows the barrage of curious questions. The conversation tends to turn to whether someone could or could not adopt, whether they want to adopt. It's like when someone says they are a vegetarian – most people automatically respond with, "I don't eat much meat." Or if someone says they don't have a TV: "Yes, I don't watch the TV much." After the questions and personal statements of whether they could or couldn't and want to or not, we get to summary comments. In some ways, it's a relief – it means the curious parent of a school friend or passenger on a plane has ran out of things to sensibly ask, and hopefully also observed your increased reluctance to spill the beans on the whole story.

You are so good.

Um, OK.

That statement rubs me up the wrong way. I know, absolutely *know*, that it is not meant to. But it does. I'll try to explain why.

From my perspective, it makes me out to be some selfless soul who sacrifices her life for the good of others. All adoptive parents have personal rationales for adopting and, while they are certainly about giving a child the love and security of a permanent family, they are usually swirled amongst adult reasons, too: I couldn't have a biological child. I fell in love with a child I met. I wanted to live a deliberately different life. I can assure you it's rarely "I wanted to be like Angelina Jolie," just for the record.

So my choice to adopt was a result of a range of reasons, but don't make me out to be some selfless soul I am not.

From the perspective of our children, the implication is that they are less desirable; that it was a hard decision to "take them on" and "give them a better life". It was, in fact, the easiest decision we've ever made, and while they drive me bonkers, I think they are the most awesome children in the world. Both statements sound much like any other mother. When people make some kind of comment in the line of "you're so good" with my kids in earshot, it makes me plain sad.

◆ ◆ ◆

As an adoptive or foster parent, I guarantee you will get the *You're so good* commentary. The trick is in how to deal with it.

I've muddled through a few approaches:

◊ Bumbling embarrassment: I don't know what you mean, I haven't done anything much... Blush, cringe, leave.

◈   Cranky: I don't think I'm good at all, here are all the reasons why. Self-deprecating comments. Blush, leave.

◈   Deflective: either onto the speaker (I'm sure you'd be a great adoptive parent too) or the children (I am the lucky one, they are the best things that have ever happened to me). Leave.

With some years of experience under my belt, though, I realise that what the person is really trying to say is, I support you and your family and your choices, and wish you all the best. But that all sounds a bit emo to say to a stranger or acquaintance.

Sometimes the best and most gracious response, given that most of the time the intention behind the comment is good, is to smile and say nothing. Pick your battles, my friends. This ain't one of them.

When Your Baby
Doesn't Come Home

A fter one of our rounds of paperwork was finally completed, we
were referred a little girl, aged 20 months. I'd been so excited to
get a referral, and heard my adoptive mother friends talk about how
they felt a quick connection, a protectiveness, a love for their child-
to-be just from their photo. For me, this was weird. I am generally
a highly emotional person, but I looked at her photo and felt no
connection to this child who was to be our daughter. I trusted this
would resolve itself, though, and we started to prepare for her arrival.

We started the waiting game, for the next important phone call
or email to let us know we should fly over for the court case. But we
never got that call. Instead, the children's centre called to advise us
that her "dead" birth mother had appeared and wanted her back.
While this sounds perverse to Western ears, it's apparently fairly
common for a father to give the child up for adoption, stating that
the birth mother is deceased. With little official documentation kept
in many countries, authorities simply question as many people as
possible to verify the story. As it turned out, this one wasn't true.

We were disappointed and let down, yet somehow I had a feeling
it was for the best. A couple of months later, I was flicking through a
packet of photos from a friend's trip to the same children's centre and

saw a photo of a little baby boy that stopped me in my tracks. I stared at the photo for the longest time. I felt deep within me that I knew this child, and that he was going to be our son. I asked her about the boy, but she didn't know anything about him. I was full of emotion and excitement; I somehow knew that he would be our son.

After weeks of waiting impatiently, the centre staff emailed and confirmed that the boy was available for adoption, and asked if we would like to adopt him. YES!!! As opposed to the earlier referral where, for whatever reason, I didn't feel much, I knew *this was our boy*. My husband and I were so enthusiastic and excited in our preparations. From that point, nothing could be done fast enough. I wanted my baby in my arms. After months of staring at photos of him, and madly refreshing my email inbox, we were anticipating the call to tell us to fly over for the court case.

When we received a call, they said he was dead.

Our baby was dead. Our little boy.

I screamed. I couldn't understand. I talked and cried and talked and cried. Friends came around to play with the kids and hug me. My husband ranged between utterly hopeless and angry, and gardened and shovelled his pain away. He needed to transfer his rage and hurt into hard labour.

I couldn't believe that instead of sorting out his paperwork to return home, I was organising a headstone.

I couldn't believe that this little boy, who I knew with all my heart was meant to be our son, was never going to be in our arms.

He died in the orphanage, with our arrival literally days away, not knowing he had a family who loved him dearly and would have done anything to show him that love, to care for him, to simply hold him as he slipped away.

I ached for him. For a child I somehow felt I knew, a child I loved, our son.

We grieved hard and long for our boy. A boy we never met, who we were not able to help. It was hard for many of our friends and family members to understand. Probably just like the insensitive comments you get after a miscarriage: just try again, it wasn't meant to be. Bullshit.

After what felt like forever, but was probably only a few months, we decided to continue.

I *did* want to adopt another child. I ached and ached. I was moody, and my insides felt hollow, but I knew I still wanted to do what we had set out to do.

After a few misunderstandings with the same centre, we decided to start afresh in another country. As soon as we began the new process, it felt smoother and more reliable. We were referred another seven-month-old boy quite quickly. We accepted the referral, and while my husband was very excited, I was scared and highly cautious. I felt empty. I didn't feel connected to this little boy. I looked at his photo and tried to feel some sort of emotion.

My husband encouraged me to visit him at the children's centre during the adoption process. I was dubious. *What if it doesn't work out? What if he doesn't end up being our son? What if he dies, too?*

Then my husband asked me: "Wouldn't you have loved to have spent some time, *any* time, with our boy before he died?" Yes. The answer was a huge *yes*. That was all I had wanted – to hold him, and look deep into his eyes. I'd wanted him to know that he was loved.

So yes, I would go to the children's centre. Even if I was shaking with apprehension, I would go and spend time with this baby boy. I would hold him, and maybe love him. I am the most open-hearted person; I love most people I know. I do not scare easily. I was attacked by a dog when I was a child, and have still spent the rest of my life having dogs and loving them. But this pain I had felt, losing our boy, had scarred me. I was closed off, scared to love this new baby. But I would try.

I booked my ticket and off I went, laden with things for the centre and for the baby. I was nervous, a little excited and pretty frazzled. The two-and-a-half-hour car journey to the centre was excruciating. My adrenaline managed to keep pumping throughout the entire trip. I videoed the last part of the journey, so I could show my husband and other children. As the car pulled in, I jumped out before it had even come to a complete stop. A nanny from the centre was walking around with a baby on her hip. It was him. He was tiny.

I was so shocked to see just how small this little baby was. My heart melted. Our tiny baby boy. She handed him to me, and I cried. I held him in my arms and just couldn't believe I was lucky enough to get to hold him, see him, smell him, touch him.

No matter what happened after that, I knew I would always be grateful that I was brave enough to go and see him. Even though the paperwork hadn't yet gone through, even though there was a chance things wouldn't work out, I was lucky. I got to meet and hold this gorgeous little human.

Luckily for me, the third time was the charm. Four months later, we walked into our house holding our legally adopted son.

◆ ◆ ◆

Here is some advice for preparing yourself for the potential of a failed adoption:

◊ People will tell you not to get too attached during the adoption process. There is always a chance that things could go wrong (particularly when dealing with developing countries). But there was nothing I could do about my love for and attachment to our son who died. I loved him from the moment I saw that photo of him, and even though we experienced great pain and loss, we also experienced that love. And for that, I am grateful.

◊ When you are going through the process, healthy detachment would be ideal, but once you have received your referral, I say dive straight in. Love that child and be joyous in your anticipation. Each moment of that is a gift in and of itself. I know the process is long and hard, but it is part of your journey, so stop and appreciate each part of it. It is a small moment of time that is about you and your child. Not getting attached during the process is like being pregnant and not being happy because of your fear of miscarriage. Try hard to let go of the understandable fear, and simply love.

◊ Writing a journal can be helpful, particularly when things don't go the way you planned. Writing about your fears, sadness, hopes, dreams, your every emotion is a fantastic and healthy release.

◈ People will not understand your loss. People who have not gone through the adoption process will not get that you loved the child, or that you were so attached to the child. They will say, "At least you hadn't met him," or "Oh well, just adopt another child." People who have suffered miscarriage or stillbirth, or have been through adoption, will be your greatest comfort. Those closest to you will hopefully understand how great your loss is. But if not, recognise that they have never experienced anything like this, and they just don't understand. And that's OK.

◈ Loss is a part of life. Learning to let go and move forward is the hardest part of loving, but once you have, you will accept life as a journey in which the only certainty is impermanence. Try to enjoy the transience of life, and love endlessly.

The Central Issue: Trauma

———◇———

"Adoption is grief in reverse."
Jody Cantrell Dyer

———◇———

Section Contents

Introduction

During our preparation to adopt, whether in the counselling sessions or our own reading (back in the days when we could still sit and read a book), we focused on attachment and its potential malfunctions in an adopted child. We quickly understood that helping our children to form a secure attachment to us was our most important job.

What we missed in our early research, though, was a robust understanding of the root of attachment issues being the child's initial trauma. Developmental trauma refers to a specific type of complex trauma that primarily focuses on the effects on a child who experiences abuse or neglect early in life.

Developmentally traumatised children are at high risk of facing challenges with attachment, health, emotional regulation, dissociation, behavioural/impulse control, cognition and self-concept.

For absolute clarity, understand that our belief is that the critical issue is trauma. Trauma has a range of potential impacts, with attachment issues being one grouping.

Having had secure and happy childhoods, we read the words and took in concepts around attachment (and trauma), but didn't *really* understand what we had to deal with until we were in the thick of adoptive parenting. When we started out, we truly believed that if you loved your child enough, you could compensate for their trauma and loss.

Over ten years into our adoption journeys, each of our kids has been with us for far longer than they were anywhere else. It can be hard to accept that the loss of birth parents is so primal, so beyond words, that even if they were only with them for weeks, or months, or didn't even know them beyond birth, the scar is still deep and permanent. The pain from this loss rears its head viciously and unexpectedly. It often manifests itself as anger towards you as the adoptive parent. It becomes *your* fault. It doesn't matter that you didn't cause this separation or this loss; you're the living, breathing permanent reminder of it.

One of the most painful realisations of adoptive parenting is that your love isn't enough to fill the hole. Adopted children have been deeply traumatised and that pain will stay with them, sometimes front of mind and sometimes barely noticeable, through their whole lives. The loss of, or inability to live with, your birth family is not something that just goes away, and at stressful or milestone moments in their lives, it will become front and centre for them again. Your love is absolutely enough, though, and absolutely critical to ensuring they get the help and support they need to move through their trauma.

Introduction to Trauma

The starting point to understanding your child is to acknowledge that, without question, he or she has suffered an emotional trauma. This can be difficult to accept, but we believe it is universally true of adopted children. You, the adoptive parents, are the ones who must deal with it, or at least find a way of helping the child to manage it so that it does not become an all-encompassing, chronic cause of economic, social, relationship and health issues.

What is a trauma? It is any event or series of events that overwhelms a person's capacity to process and cope, physically, mentally and emotionally. These events cause a rupture in the normative development of the mind-body. The trauma might be neglect, abandonment or abuse, for example.

This experience has changed the child, who has adapted in order to survive. This adaptation made perfect sense at the time, but now the child cannot move on from this mode of adaptation, even post-adoption. It is one thing for them to cognitively understand that their new family loves them, that they are safe and that it is not necessary to continue with the survival adaptation (though this realisation is hard enough for a child), it is quite another for the child to truly *feel* safe enough to let go of what has been a successful strategy thus far.

The adaption necessary to survive the trauma can become a permanent state of dysregulation. Often a child uses up most of their energy simply trying to survive post-trauma. This leaves very little energy or opportunity for learning, positive relational interaction, developing a sense of self and identity, and fully experiencing all the things that a child of their age would typically do.

◆   ◆   ◆

I cannot stress enough the importance of having some understanding of brain development following a trauma in childhood. Investing time in understanding trauma is crucial for parents, as it allows you to replace frustration with empathy.

Many things about your child's behaviour may be perplexing and, possibly, quite infuriating. Why are they always chewing stuff? Why can't they follow simple instructions? What's with the tight clothes? Why are they playing with baby toys? Why are they so uncoordinated? Why do they do things that they know they shouldn't? How do they know all the words to the latest songs on the radio, but can't remember their times tables? Why are they so impulsive? Why do they get up in the middle of the night to take food? Why are they stealing and stashing food? Why do they get so upset about minor things? I am sure you have observed many other behavioural issues that seem strange and unfathomable.

Some of these behaviours can be explained through a deeper understanding of how the child's brain develops in response to trauma. There are many excellent books in this area, and I highly recommend that you take a look at the work of Dr Bruce Perry of the Child Trauma Academy, who wrote *The Boy Who Was Raised As A Dog*,[6] and Bessel van der Kolk's *The Body Keeps The Score*.[7]

This topic can appear highly complex and limitless, but

---

6 *The Boy Who Was Raised as a Dog: And Other Stories from a Child Psychiatrist's Notebook–What Traumatized Children Can Teach Us About Loss, Love, and Healing*, Bruce Perry & Maia Szalavitz

7 *The Body Keeps the Score: Brain, Mind, and Body in the Healing of Trauma*, Bessel van der Kolk M.D.

you only need to go as deep as you want. The model that I have found most helpful is again from Dr Bruce Perry, and is called the Neurosequential Model of Therapeutics (NMT).[8] This is neither a treatment nor a diagnosis, but a framework that plots a child's neurological development and compares it to a "neurotypical" child of the same age. The premise is that a child's brain needs to develop in a particular sequence, and trauma can interrupt that sequence, thereby skewing their development. Each child adapts to survive his or her particular traumatic circumstances, and this can cause the sequence of development to be disturbed or incomplete.

Depending on the situation, the impact of trauma may be evident from day one, with the child exhibiting tantrums, rage, violence and dissociation after even a trivial interaction. Or nothing may manifest for years, until the additional burdens of school, friends and puberty overwhelm their survival mechanisms and they suddenly start to struggle. By looking at when and what happened, and the child's subsequent survival strategy, we can hypothesise which parts of the brain may have been affected, and then seek targeted therapies to enable the brain to complete its development.

It is possible to have your child assessed for an NMT "mind map" that can give you insight into areas where your child is relatively stronger or weaker compared to a typically neuro-developed child. This then allows you to target activities that will help your child the most, for where they are at that time. It is pointless having a maths tutor, for example, if your child has not developed the neurological structures necessary to enable them to access the higher levels of abstract thought and logic. Your child might need other occupational therapy-type activities first. An NMT assessment can give you a framework to target therapies (where "therapy", in this context, is simply a beneficial activity, eg. skipping or one-on-one play). See the Child Trauma Academy's website for more information about NMT, including where to find a practitioner in your area.[9] The website also has educational articles and presentations you can download for free.

---

8 http://childtrauma.org/nmt-model/

9 www.childtrauma.org

◆   ◆   ◆

The earlier in life that trauma occurs, the more likely it is that basic
-level functioning will be affected. By age two, a child's brain is 75% of
its adult size, and by age six, it has reached 90%. This means that the
impact of trauma at age ten is going to be very different to a trauma at
age one. If we understand that, say, trauma occurred at a time typically
associated with sensory development, we would not be surprised to
find that the child has sensory input difficulties, movement problems
and issues processing sensory data. How this manifests is unique to
that child. It could be in gait, balance, sight, touch, perception of
space, motor skills, etc. In this scenario, targeted trauma-enlightened
occupational therapy is your best friend. Using targeted OT, we can
harness neuroplasticity to complete the development of sensory
processing. This then frees the child from having to spend so much
energy and attention on the body. It also enables them to make
stronger connections to other parts of the brain, and to move towards
a more typical neuro-biological level of functioning.

If a child is primarily dysregulated at a sensory level and frequents
the fight/flight/freeze state, she will often be unable to use her own
cognitive abilities to regulate herself – hence the *How many times
have I told you?* exasperation for parents. When a child is calm and
feels safe, she can access her cognitive abilities and agree that a
particular course of action is unwise. However, once the child feels
stress, she literally cannot access that part of the brain. The fight/
flight/freeze reaction dominates, to the exclusion of rational thinking.

A child who has experienced trauma will have the same brain
structure that everyone else of their age has, of course. But the issue
is how to move past, in this case, sensory dominations over rational
thinking. Talking therapies seek to access the cognitive part of the
brain – the rational thinking part that is difficult to access for these
children. As a result, talking therapies, while useful and illuminating,
can be an exasperatingly slow way to facilitate change.

This approach seeks to complete the neuro-development that
has been interrupted by the trauma-enforced adaptation. It does so

through trauma-enlightened, targeted activities (in this scenario, we were considering a child with sensory input issues – OT is not the answer for everyone, but the fundamental methodology is the same). This means we can attempt to redirect the brain's focus and energy on the body and the fight/flight/freeze response towards building stronger neural connections with the cognitive system. In time, this will mean that talking therapy is more effective and will increase the child's ability to self-regulate (in other words, make good decisions when you are not there!).

◆   ◆   ◆

Understanding trauma and its impact on your child's brain also helps you to parent them with empathy and understanding. If you know your child craves sensory input because his brain has not completed a neurotypical development, you are less likely to get annoyed when your 12-year-old climbs into a tiny space under the sofa and stays there. If you understand that pressure is a calming thing for your child, instead of having a bedtime routine of soothing music and stories, you might want to wrestle with your child.

In addition, if you understand that your child is living in an emotional space controlled by hypervigilance that stems from a permanently "on" sense of danger, then you will reasonably expect that they will not be accessing the rational, forward-thinking part of the brain. They may not understand even the simplest of instructions, or you may have to repeat them more than you think is necessary. They may be quicker to take offence to small things, and become argumentative and sullen.

You need to become experts in your child's psychological rehabilitation. While you can get excellent support, you cannot outsource this to psychologists, psychiatrists, respite carers, counsellors or anyone else. It's up to you. This is not an easy job. It will take many years of concerted effort, and put great strain on you personally, as well as on your relationships with your partner, your children and your family.

For some foundational reading on attachment and trauma, we list our favourite books in the resources section of our website.[10] Read these for the theory, and read our stories that follow to understand you're not alone, and to find the practical tips and strategies that resonate with your family.

---

10 www.lionheartfamilies.com/resources

General Strategies Around Attachment Issues

Dealing with attachment issues can be devastating. You will often feel hopeless and helpless and clueless and just *less* – you never thought it was going to be *this* hard. You had no idea that not only would you feel you were having little impact but that, at times, your very presence would seem to be making your child's issues worse.

Dealing with attachment issues is isolating. Many people in the broader community have no idea of the challenges you face inside your home day in, day out. We had no idea of the hard work we would all have to put in over years to shift the dial for our kids, even a little.

Remember, attachment issues stemming from trauma are areas where you need to bring in the big guns. Read the books from qualified professionals, get help from your family doctor (but make sure they have trauma and attachment experience, or they'll tell you "It's just kids"), psychologists, psychiatrists, whatever you need.

It takes a huge amount of patience and understanding to parent a child who lacks the basic foundations of a secure attachment. A child who feels "unsafe" often struggles with basic family concepts.

They'll often exhibit negative behaviours, they might always question authority and the purpose of rules, and will rarely self-reflect. All of these behaviours add up to children that are very challenging to parent.

Solutions and effective techniques will depend largely on their history, their developmental age and also their cognitive and chronological age. All children learn differently, and all parents parent differently, so there is not one solution that fits all. The majority of children who have suffered disruption in childhood have a distorted and faulty perception that they are bad, not worthy, not good enough. With this in mind, a child may subconsciously believe that "I am bad, so what's the point in being good and changing the way I act."

As humans, we behave in a way that supports our primary beliefs about ourselves and others. For example, a child may believe that they are only "good" when they have your undivided attention, so they do everything possible to get it, even if it's negative. You screaming and shouting at them is giving them attention and, in their eyes, this is what they want. They may feel that when you correct them, you do not love them. If we, as parents, do not highlight and correct these faulty beliefs, then standard parenting techniques will not work. Most parenting strategies assume that a child's core beliefs are positive, and therefore they work for your "standard" child. But a child with faulty beliefs is inspired by very different choices, and therefore views and interprets the world very differently.

Attachment to a primary caregiver can alter these beliefs, but it's not a quick process. A family counsellor who is experienced in trauma and attachment is likely to work with your family on strengthening parent-to-child bonds through life story work, active discussion and parenting with Patience, Acceptance, Curiosity and Empathy (PACE),[11] rather than dealing with the actual behaviours. As the child becomes safer and more secure, the behaviours tend to diminish or subside, and relationships become easier to heal.

Below, we list some general observations and strategies that will help you as you try to understand your child, and work with them to feel safe and secure in your family.

---

11 This is a technique that has been developed by Dan Hughes, a leading authority on attachment and trauma.

◈ No matter the age of the child, or your sense of how well-adjusted they are, assume when you first parent them that they are scared, confused and grieving for another place, a centre, a foster family, a birth family. Give your family time and space to become established before adding lots of other people to the mix.

◈ Think of how much attention babies receive – they are held, fed, tickled, smiled at, talked to. They are constantly on the receiving end of a whole lot of love from the world at large. Institutionalised kids don't get this. They sit in cots and are fed and changed, but little else. When they can walk, they wander around with other kids, in a situation that sometimes verges on resembling *Lord of the Flies*. It is hard to understand the profound impact of this. I suggest that the best way to learn what it was like to be your child as an infant is to read *Building the Bonds of Attachment*.[12] Reading this allowed me to make sense of my child's infancy and early years.

◈ Often the children are more comfortable with negative attention because it matches their faulty belief system. It's also more intense for them, and generally undivided. Emotional regulation is difficult for these children and therefore they can become frequently overwhelmed with strong emotions that cause blockages in their coping strategies. These blockages, in turn, create a need for control. Control is often a massive concern for them. Not only do they feel that they need to control situations, but they can also become very self-reliant, take care of themselves and rarely ask for help. This habit can be hard to break and may lead to increased anxiety and defiance, which in turn feeds the need for control.

◈ Regulating the child's emotions, establishing a more connected relationship, and giving your child frequent opportunities to accomplish things can begin to combat these negative beliefs.

◈ For every negative thing you say to your child, find three positive things to say, too. With children suffering from trauma, it is easy to spend most of your time saying "no" or other negative comments

---

12 *Building the Bonds of Attachment, Awakening Love in Deeply Troubled Children*, Daniel A. Hughes.

– don't do that, stop that, etc. I read years ago that you should aim to say three positive things for every negative. This might seem a challenge at times, but the three positive things don't have to be major. It could be praise for listening, completing a task, doing something for someone else, not getting into trouble at school, or a success in some activity. Try not to link the positives and negatives in a "compliment sandwich" – don't just say positive things because you are about to say something negative. Try and find positive things to praise all the time. You will be surprised by how responsive your child is to praise.[13]

◈ Try not to start with a positive and then set an expectation. For example: "See how well you behaved today at granny's house. Now let's see if we can do that next week, too." It's important to praise the moment. Don't finish it with an expectation for next time, as this just sets them up for failure again, and instils the feeling of "I'm never good enough."

◈ All children need boundaries and discipline in order to learn how to navigate life. Many children with disrupted attachments read verbal and non-verbal signs incorrectly. They often wrongly interpret things as negative because of their own negative belief system. For example, telling them "We are leaving soon" may be immediately met with a "Why?" response, as if you're punishing them (when you simply need to pick up a sibling at 3pm). By giving warnings, managing expectations and being consistent, a child will learn to accept authority a lot easier. So this simple request could be phrased as follows: "Just to let you know that we need to collect your brother at 3pm," or "I'm hoping to leave at about 3pm today," or "Do you think you can be ready to head out in ten minutes?"

◈ Remember that their chronological age is often older than their developmental age. Trying to reason with a 12-year-old who is arguing with her two-year-old sister about who gets the yellow cup is frustrating and tiring. When we expect them to act their

13 Except in the beginning of your relationship, when praising them could cause them to stop and do the exact opposite!

chronological age, the children may become overwhelmed (which may, in turn, present as oppositional behaviour). Try to observe and evaluate your child's actions separately from her chronological age to find parenting strategies that will work for her as she is now.

◈ Be consistent! *Always* follow through with what you say. Children need to know and understand consequences: "What will happen if I do this?" By following through, you keep your word and establish a boundary that will help your child feel more secure and safe in your presence. You cannot be one of these parents who threatens and doesn't follow through.

◈ Don't give up. What doesn't work today, may work tomorrow. Children move through different developmental stages. As they mature, different parenting strategies may start to work even if they were not initially successful. For example, logical and natural consequences may not be understood by a child who believes she does not deserve good things, or work for a child who is developmentally like a two-year-old – an age at which autonomy may be more important than self-benefit. However, as she gets more attached to you and revises her core beliefs, it may become a successful parenting method.

◈ Be upfront and clear about your good intentions. One way to defuse negative interpretations is to be explicit. For example, if you answer a phone call from a friend and your child starts constantly interrupting the conversation, instead of getting mad and gesturing for them to go away, ask your friend to give you 30 seconds. Tell your child: "You are interrupting a conversation. I want to hear what you have to say, and I will be more interested once I've had this phone call with my friend. It would be better if you wait quietly until I finish this conversation. I will then ask you what you want and I will listen to what you have to say." This is hugely draining, time-consuming and so repetitive. It can, however, defuse the child and you can usually see an immediate change. Other times, it may not work, but consistency will pay off if you remain in control.

◈ A phrase we have learned to rely on throughout our parenting journey is "everyone does something for a rational, logical reason." I find it helpful to always come back to this when one of the kids is behaving in a way I don't understand. I accept that there is an underlying reason for it, and trust that at some point, whether tomorrow or next year, I will understand it. It takes some of the "why" pressure off today, and allows you to work on the issue at hand in a more practical and less intellectual way. Of course, if you can already pinpoint the "why," it makes the response a whole lot more likely to succeed.

◈ Acting on impulse as a parent is doing exactly what children do with their negative actions. **We need to learn to think and regulate ourselves before dealing with incidents.** This looks silly bolded, but it is absolutely critical.

◈ Don't take attachment issues personally. This involves you, yes, but it's not *about* you and it's certainly nothing to do with your parenting abilities. If you take it personally, your child will feel they can't discuss their feelings with you, for fear of upsetting you. Your child needs to know you will hear their pain without judgement or ego. Help them to name and understand their feelings. Tell them it's OK to be angry, that every child should have the opportunity of being raised by their biological parents, and that it *is* sad that they do not. Hug them.

◈ Don't assume that kids will want to heal by talking. In fact, as explained in the section on trauma, talking will often prove pointless for kids who can't access their faculties of higher thinking. Some of our kids function best when we allow them distraction when they're really sad. For them, talking only adds more pain, and watching a movie about something else altogether makes them feel better. Also, doing something together, like making biscuits or drawing pictures, allows some space for the child to safely process their feelings and is likely to lead to a more useful conversation for both of you.

◈ We each sent our kids to day-care or preschool close to when they were "supposed" to go. With hindsight, we believe that kids who have been institutionalised are likely to do better and develop more rapidly if they're kept at home for as long as it's practical (or as long as you can bear it!). Intense time at home, learning who's who in the family, will help bonds to form faster, without confusing them by introducing other caregivers. The kids are also likely to get more from school in terms of learning and social interaction if they have had some adjustment time at home.

◈ All that said, institutionalised kids typically have behavioural issues that are hard to deal with. With some of our kids, the hours they were at nursery or preschool were precious snippets of time that allowed us to recover. If you need to put the kids into care for whatever reason, do it without guilt.

◈ When an older child is adopted, they will often decide to be "good": to lap up the love bestowed upon them, to try not cause trouble, to fill up with praise that they've never had before. One of my children was "good", though perhaps not true to herself, for over five years.

◈ Parenting a child with attachment issues can be extremely hard work and hugely draining, not to mention very isolating. Be kind to yourself, and look after your own wellbeing. Do not parent in isolation. Your support network becomes your lifeline during these times. We don't always admit to it, but there are other parents feeling exactly as you are right now.

In the end, there is no single parenting strategy that will be the answer for a successful relationship with your child.

The Early Days
of Attachment

In the early days after bringing our baby girl home, I was very careful not to have visitors in the house. No family came to stay, and playdates and coffees were all arranged outside of the house. I wanted to create a sanctuary for our new girl. Her home was just us. It was safe.

It was to be expected that our friends, who were excited to meet our new baby, bristled at my approach. I had arguments with family members about my being too protective. Even after those first few weeks, when I eventually allowed them to visit, I would not let them hold her, feed her or put her to bed. It was hard, but it was right. She was scared, and it was our job to soothe and comfort her.

Because I was young, a new parent, and perhaps also because I had just met our baby, I wasn't as forceful as I should have been about following my instincts. I was told so many times that I shouldn't rock her to sleep as it creates bad habits, or that she shouldn't still be eating pureed food at 12 months, or that I needed to let her cry, because it was good for her. I worked hard to stick to my guns and let this advice wash over me, but the comments did have an impact on me.

I found it frustrating – in fact, I still do – that other parents judge our girl and our parenting of her based on their biological parenting yardsticks. I have learned that, yes, many things *are* the same however your child comes to you, but parenting a baby who was both desperately ill and emotionally scarred *is* different in a lot of ways. I am a biological and adoptive parent, and I can tell you from firsthand experience, they are not the same.

◆ ◆ ◆

Here are some tips for the early days:

◊ When you're preparing to bring your child home, tell people well ahead of time how you plan on handling the first few weeks, and thank them in advance for their understanding. In fact, to help you out, we have created an electronic guide for friends and families of newly adopted children. You can access it on our website[14] and share it with your loved ones. It also lists further reading.

◊ Social media and email can be helpful in the early days. A photo and an update will soothe the frustration your family and friends will feel at having limited contact.

◊ When you feel like your child is ready for more interaction, start small. Limit large social events upon your child's return home. Your child is scared and needs peace and time to build a bond with you, not your 20 best friends. Big "welcome home" bashes will scare the shit out of them. Sorry, we know how exciting it is to finally bring your child home and how much you want to celebrate. But just hold your horses, for the sake of your child.

◊ Follow your instincts with your child. You don't need to have birthed a child, or parented them for an eon, to have a sense of what is best for them.

---

14 www.lionheartfamilies.com/resources

When Loving
Is Scary

While we arranged the adoption paperwork, I was able to visit the centre and meet our nine-month-old boy. The second I met him and held him, I melted. He was beautiful. I fed him, rocked him to sleep, stared at him, and quickly fell in love. He stared back, confused. He was not used to such intense attention, but started to adjust in the days we had together.

I had to return to Dubai without him and wait for the paperwork to be finalised. After only two months, we got the green light to pick him up. We'd had a few false starts in our adoption journey, and this had all gone so smoothly that it felt almost too good to be true.

The day we picked him up went wonderfully. We played with him and fed him at the centre, and after he seemed more comfortable with us, we took him in the car to the city hotel two-and-a-half hours away. He seemed a little confused, but fell asleep peacefully and woke up at the hotel full of smiles.

He seemed to be a happy little boy. He immediately learned to crawl and pull himself up on things (after being kept in a cot every day since birth). He laughed and smiled all day. He was getting used to me feeding him, instead of independently holding his bottle. He loved eye contact and stimulation. He was slowly able to eat a little solid food, as long as I was singing and dancing to distract him while I secretly slipped it into his mouth!

For the first couple of months, I was blissfully exhausted and so happy to have our little boy at home with us. This tiny baby needed so much love and help, and we were going to give it all to him. I think, like every adoptive parent, we wanted to love him so much that the early, hard months of his life would fade over time.

A major challenge was his inability to cuddle. He had never been held, and he didn't know how to relax his body and mould to me. He couldn't relax his limbs enough to cuddle up close; in fact, the whole concept was absolutely alien to him.

Whenever he was tired, our interactions would quickly deteriorate. I would instinctively try to actively put him to sleep – to hold him, rock him and stroke him to let him know he was safe and loved. It seemed to me that he wanted this, too, but didn't know how to accept my affection. If I tried to cuddle him, he would arch his back and scream. If I put him down in his cot, he would arch his back and scream. He wanted me, and he wanted love, but he was confused.

We found our middle ground. I held him facing me, one hand behind his neck, allowing him to arch backwards, while rocking him side to side and singing. Slowly, very slowly, but surely, he would drift off to sleep and his body would start to relax. I would bring him closer to me bit by bit, until at last, he would be asleep on my chest. Amazing. Besides my aching arms and back, it felt wonderful. This process took about 45 minutes each time.

In general, he found the stimulation of everyday life overwhelming, having been deprived of stimulation in his earliest months. While he appeared excited to be given love and attention, he also seemed scared it would stop as abruptly as it had started. He would fall asleep after my backache-inducing rocking, only to wake within an hour. Every single sleep. Day or night.

When he did wake, no matter what I did to comfort him, he would push against me and scream. As I felt myself getting frustrated, I would start to leave the room, but that only made him scream louder. I wanted to love and comfort him so that he could sleep. I was sad that the one thing that would result in him sleeping was me getting so frustrated that I would yell, *"Just go to sleep!"* It upset me that the only thing that would relax him was yelling. How could a baby take comfort from yelling? It became a horrible cycle of me trying to be kind, him not responding, then me yelling and him relaxing.

I knew that he needed patience and persistence, and I was not surprised or upset by this wakefulness. I understood that there would be a transition period and that he would not find comfort in me for a while, so I would reassure him and rub, rock or feed him every time he woke. I wanted him to know that we were his family, and that he could rely on us to take care of him. After two months of this loving behaviour not helping or being accepted, I started to feel hopeless. My intensive efforts at being his perfect mother, combined with our lack of sleep, saw me end up unwell, and absolutely exhausted.

◆　◆　◆

My early days with him made me realise how reciprocal a mother-child relationship is. With my biological kids, I had done absolutely everything for them without complaint in the early days. I didn't realise until we were parenting our boy that even as tiny infants, they had given me a lot in return. If they cried, I would cuddle or stroke them and they would eventually stop. When I looked at them with love, they would mirror a loving look back to me. Our relationships were a blissful dance between loving people.

With my baby boy, things were incredibly different. I would look at him with love and try to be gentle and caring, but his responses were unpredictable. This tiny baby was full of confusion, frustration, and anger.

At night, I would hold him against my naked chest while giving him his bottle. I wanted him to have the skin-to-skin experience a breastfed baby gets. I wanted him to feel close and connected to me. Sometimes he would relax and settle in; other times, he would stare at me, this tiny baby, with real anger in his eyes and slap me. Hard. He would hit my face, my chest, anywhere. He would hit me so hard that it shocked me. I would stroke his arm and tell him he was my baby and that I loved him, and it was OK to be angry.

Looking back, this was the only time in the day I allowed him to feel his emotions fully, without trying to modify them. I can now see that these were emotions I was uncomfortable with, that made me feel challenged and powerless. It scared me that he had such strong emotions, emotions I labelled as being negative. I tried to paper over them, to suppress them. I wanted to make him happy, and every time that didn't work, my fear would kick in and I would start to feel angry.

I wanted so much for this child to be comforted by me. To some extent, he was – he would cling to me and call, again and again, *"Mama, Mama."* But when he cried because he was scared, confused, angry or frustrated, I couldn't make him relax. I couldn't take away his pain. This killed me.

I had prided myself on being a calm, loving mother. I had no idea that I had a deep need to see my children feeling happy. I realise now how negatively I viewed anger and frustration. I hadn't realised that when I set out to adopt a child, part of it was about "fixing" a broken child. I had so much love to give, and I thought I could love a baby until he was whole again.

My husband was used to me having everything under control with the children, so he was shocked by my inability to deal with our boy and the sleeplessness and angst. He was also shocked that I started mirroring the baby's aggression back to him. When I would be at the height of frustration after he had woken ten times that night, I would hold our boy's arm a little too tightly, or yell at him a little too angrily. My husband didn't know how to deal with this. I yelled at my husband that I thought I was losing it, and he nodded his head. He was worried about me and the kids. It was like someone stabbing me straight through the heart. It was my worst nightmare.

I tried and tried every single day. I would wake up and think, today I will be kind and gentle. I did every practical thing I could think of: I took our boy to a cranial osteopath and an occupational therapist; he had a weighted blanket and other sensory tools to help with his sensory issues; he had grommets inserted as he hadn't been able to hear well; he had his tongue-tie snipped; I massaged him. I was doing everything I could to live up to my expectations of myself as a mother. But I was still failing. I had no compassion for myself. I was frustrated and disappointed in myself.

I would question why this was happening. This child was teaching me to become bad. I had set out to do something good – so why was I being punished? Of course, we'd have a few good moments each day, but generally I felt shaky, angry and a failure.

◆ ◆ ◆

When our fourth child was born, the other three children, my husband and my sister were all present. There was of course the great joy that comes with new life. But the most wonderful part was the love that our prickly boy instantly showed for his baby brother. He gazed at him with love and amazement – just like I did. He didn't want to let him go. He loved being a big brother, and he was wonderful at it.

Each moment of our newborn's day was spent with people loving him, holding him, kissing him, talking to him, feeding him. It reminded me how much our adopted boy had missed out on in his first 11 months of life. I had known it rationally before, but the gravity of him being denied the constant attention, love and tenderness that creates a person's self-worth really hit me. I realised that deep inside him, there was no sense of self-worth. He didn't love himself, and therefore couldn't love me.

The next couple of years were difficult. I struggled to be kind to myself, and remained frustrated and tough on our boy. I went to a psychologist who, during my hour-and-a-half session, said one thing that made the situation absolutely crystal clear for the first time: "You keep trying to fix him, and you can't. You don't have to. He is who he is. That first year of his life is part of him, and you need to accept that and let him be."

For years, I hadn't really understood the extent to which I had been pushing back against that fact. I had been trying to force our boy to skip over his negative emotions, to be a happy, contented child, and then punishing myself for not being able to fix him, not being able to make him whole. What a release to hear those words that day! I cried and cried.

This moment of clarity liberated my parenting of him. I had been unhappy with the situation, and all I had to do was look at it differently. I had to let go. I had to accept him for who he was, and accept myself as I was. I know it all makes sense and seems logical, but when I was in the situation, I just couldn't see what I was doing. My little boy has taught me more than anyone or anything else in my life.

One night, when he had been with us for six years, he woke up distressed. I went into him, stroked his face and told him he was safe. He reached out and touched my face ever so gently, and said, "I love you, Mummy."

This continuing journey as his mother has opened my heart to people and situations in a different way than before. I have compassion and empathy towards other parents who are struggling. I have lost the innate impulse to judge mothers who did things that I thought were not "good enough", an impulse I wasn't even aware was there before. He continues to teach me that completely accepting yourself and others, and being kind to yourself, allows us to let go of expectations and just be ourselves.

◆　◆　◆

When an older child rejects the love you shower on them, it can sting. You might arrive to pick them up from nursery or school, and they make a big fuss about staying there and not coming with you. It's embarrassing, and you feel ashamed.

I once made this gorgeous Easter hat with my boy. He'd seen how much it had meant to me to make it for him. I asked him to put it in his bag. As we arrived at school, I asked him to get it out, and he said, with a smile, that he'd forgotten it. I remember walking home from drop-off that day, tears streaming down my face, hurt by the meanness of a child, and by what had happened to him to get him to that place. I remember feeling embarrassed when I went back for the hat parade an hour later, and everyone saw my boy in a school hat instead of an Easter hat – like I'd forgotten, rather than having spent hours the night before crafting it.

You're supposed to be this wonderful parent, and you're so focused and spending lots of time parenting and thinking about parenting. But some children will deliberately behave in a way that makes you look neglectful, and it's hurtful.

With this child, it took probably four years (yes, *four years*) to start breaking this pattern. Four years of daily, sometimes hourly rejection. It was a real story of unrequited love. Day in, day out through these years, we worked hard to show him love consistently, to display affection and care and not get angry or annoyed.

◆　◆　◆

Here are some tips on allowing your child to grieve their loss before they can accept your love:

◈ Get comfortable with allowing them to feel emotions that are negative. Don't try to paper over their feelings: speak to them about anger and sadness and missing someone, and show them it's acceptable to feel these things.

◈ Don't expect much in return from your child early on. In many cases, you will get little in the way of positive emotional responses for months or occasionally years. Fake it until you make it. Talk to your partner or friend about your frustration in getting little back, but work to stay positive with your child.

◈ Expect a lot of emotional "dancing" with your child. It's frightening for a child who has been through the trauma of losing their birth family to trust other adults, no matter how loving and consistent they are. It will scare your child when they let their guard down and love you, and they will feel vulnerable. Often, they will then behave terribly to make them feel less fearful. Stay consistent, tell them you'll always be there for them, and that you can see they feel scared and it's OK.

◈ Try to use attachment-parenting techniques as far as they make sense for you. I wish I'd used a baby carrier more with my boy, but he was big and very active. In any case, I never thought of it at the time. We've written elsewhere about our conclusion that co-sleeping is a great way to build your family bond, and each of the three of us wishes we'd practiced it at the start. Cuddle your child as much as they'll let you, even when they are like a sack of potatoes and won't hold on with their legs (in which case, sit down to cuddle them), or when they are stiff as a board and merely tolerate your hug.

◈ Expect that your child may choose to sabotage a lovely moment. You may finally be having a lovely cuddle on the couch together. Suddenly, the energy will change and you find a finger poking you hard in the face, or your child pulling your hair. Again, try to be patient. They are just demonstrating their fear of the closeness and trust they were just experiencing.

When you're in the thick of it, you might struggle to see that together, in this dance of attachment, you are inching forward two steps and back one. But you are still inching forward.

Anxiety,
Low Self-Esteem
and Depression

Some studies, including the landmark Adverse Childhood Experiences study,[15] point to children who have experienced significant trauma, including parental separation, having higher rates of anxiety and depression. I've read responses that suggest that perhaps the rates aren't really higher, but rather that parents in these cases are more likely to seek a diagnosis and counselling. I don't buy that rationale; I think it's reasonable to expect that children who have experienced trauma will sometimes struggle with their mental health.

Children with a history of trauma have an overdeveloped "fight/flight/freeze" response. Their brains can get stuck in protective mode when they sense even the smallest hint of danger.[16] This may lead

---

15 The ACE study is fascinating for many, many reasons, and central to these is the fact that this ground-breaking study is rarely used in public health. Start with the Wikipedia page, and then click through on some of the references: https://en.wikipedia.org/wiki/Adverse_Childhood_Experiences_Study

16 This fantastic booklet is useful to understanding children who instinctively go into "survival" mode: http://www.innerworldwork.co.uk/wp-content/uploads/2017/04/What-survival-looks-like...-for-me-2.pdf

them to seek control over situations, so they can feel safe.

Children whose histories include fear, numerous significant changes, or other forms of major disruption tend to be more anxious and can be more easily overwhelmed by negative emotions and environmental stimuli (like noise, light, too many people, etc.).

Research suggests that when people are highly anxious, they cannot learn. Anxiety impedes logical thinking, and for a child not skilled at logic and rational thought, even simple everyday scenarios become puzzling. Recently, for example, we were at a birthday party where cans of drink cooled in a bucket of ice. There were a variety of flavours, including cola, which our kids don't have. Our nine-year-old girl was becoming visibly agitated every time someone took a can of drink. While it's taken me a long time, I'm now more attuned to her behaviour, and I realised her brain was working overtime. I took her aside, and started the "I Wonder" spiel (a technique we explain later, in the Therapy Toolbox section) to determine if she was worried about something. She reminded me that I had once told her if you drink too much cola, your teeth can rot and fall out. She was now desperately worried that these children's teeth were going to rot and fall out right in front of her whilst they played musical statues. For her anxious brain, deciphering between fact and fiction or fantasy can be so hard.

When you have an anxious child, structure, routine and consistency are critical, as they create a sense of safety and reduce anxiety. Routine also helps us, as parents, prepare for and anticipate feelings or emotions that might arise.

In our experience, one of the best ways to help your anxious child is to reframe their anxiety. We use methods like those listed in this great Huffington Post article.[17]

◆   ◆   ◆

Our four children play and fight like all siblings do. It seems, from the outside, that everyone holds their own, each of them taking turns

---

17 http://www.huffingtonpost.com/renee-jain/9-things-every-parent-with-an-anxious-child-should-try_b_5651006.html

to say or do something nasty to the others.

One night, after a particularly shocking fight, I sat our adopted boy down to talk about his behaviour. I started off upset about how he had treated his little brother, but I could see that he was feeling dreadful. When I asked if he knew why he'd done what he had, he answered that he felt left out and like the other three didn't like him. I am always conscious of the fact we have one adopted child amongst three biological children, so I am sensitive to how he is treated.

The thing is, his three siblings adore him. They loved him from the minute we picked him up, and have treated him exactly as they would any other sibling. They do not leave him out or treat him as though they don't like him. The issue is that he doesn't actually like *himself* that much.

That night, I sat with him, cuddling and talking. He cried those horrible tears of a broken heart. He said he feels so sad and like nobody loves him. He is showered with love and affection and attention all day, every day; he just doesn't believe it. He feels a deep sense of worthlessness that causes him to not believe that we love him, no matter what we do.

I called the other kids in to talk. When my son and I told them about how he was feeling, and they saw the sadness on his face, they cried. They cried and hugged him and told him that of course they loved him, and that they were so sorry that he didn't feel that. They apologised for behaving in any way that indicated to him that they didn't love him.

This sense of not truly believing he is worthy of love rears its ugly head time and time again. If the children are having cookies, he will immediately assume that he will miss out. He has never missed out on food – we share things equally and if there isn't enough, nobody gets any. If I mention that we are going somewhere exciting, he will immediately shout out, "Even me? Do I get to come?" He never believes and trusts that he will be included and that he deserves it. If he does something silly and breaks or loses something, he will be so upset with himself, no matter how many times I tell him that we all do silly things.

His learning is tricky to manage, as it fluctuates with his feelings.

One day he will understand a maths concept and be able to do a sheet of questions. The next day, it can seem like he has never seen them before. This is due to him not being able to manage his feelings of fear. Anything can cause this anxiety: a slightly annoyed tone in my voice, his brother telling him to move, a question that looks a little tricky… His anxiety is not expressed in predictable ways. Instead, he will simply not be able to understand his work. He may flop around on his chair, moan and whine, and be very angry. This lack of consistency is improving with time, and I notice he's a little more willing to believe that he is good at things and sometimes even says nice things about himself. I can only hope that with encouragement, a few more successes and time, he will start to believe that he is enough.

In addition to anxiety and poor self-esteem, we have dealt with depression in our families. Our best advice is to work with your child to heal their trauma-related issues, while seeking professional help for mental illness. Much of the standard advice for parenting children with a mental illness applies to adoptive families, too, and we suggest you rely on these materials and methods.[18]

---

18 We like https://healthyfamilies.beyondblue.org.au as it provides information based on the child's age, and has sensible tips and links for further support.

Easy Breezy Attachment

When our boy came home, he attached differently from the start. After two weeks together with not much else to do but cuddle, play and eat "Chinese" (aka Laughing Cow Cheese), we were *so* bonded. His little face lit up as he ran to us each day. He wanted to be nowhere else but with us. It was quite heartbreaking to see how desperately this beautiful boy had needed parents.

While I was not naïve enough to think that his easy breezy attachment was because of our newly acquired parenting skills, I was quietly pleased to have an easy one, a child who wanted to be attached.

He was a beautiful child, adored by the world. Charming to adults, he would hold long conversations and stage elaborate games in our lounge.

A few weeks after we returned home, we threw him a small birthday party. He was strangely uninterested in playing with the kids, preferring to spar with an adult with a balloon sword. Even later, when friends arrived with their two little ones and we danced and sang in the lounge room together, he still wanted to interact with the parents, not the kids.

The pleasure we'd felt early on about how fabulously bonded we were was wearing off. We soon realised we were easily replaced by any other adult paying him attention. He would drop us quickly if he found another adult to give him attention.

This pattern of behaviour continued for years: we'd excitedly arrange some outing with him, only to have him ditch it if the neighbour came and asked him to do something. Or we'd be on a walk together and he'd choose to chat with a random stranger instead of spending time with us.

Even so, as the years passed by and other children struggled with various attachment issues, we felt like we had escaped any major issues with this child. He was charming and well liked, well adjusted, did OK at school given he had some learning challenges, attached to us and spoke to us when something was wrong.

Then we pulled the rug out from under him by moving the children's schools, exposing the fact that his self-esteem and relationships were a house of cards. And did they ever come crashing down.

He felt like he stuck out in the new school, that he was different from the others in so many ways. He tried to be a chameleon and adapt, but it was fairly pointless. He spent most of the school year alone at lunchtime, with just one friend. He showed great fortitude in continuing to turn up and read his book at lunchtime, as a means of tolerating these new conditions.

And then came the start of high school. He went without a fuss, but remained frustrated that it was taking him a while to make friends. He had lived on a front of charm his whole life and now, for the last year, it had stopped working. His self-esteem continued to deteriorate and we started to realise that he was suffering anxiety and depression. We had to intervene quickly, as well as seek help for him.

◆　◆　◆

Here are some tips for managing kids who attach too easily:

◈　Try to understand that this attachment style has been a means of survival for them. This child of ours spent the most years of any of our kids in care. In a children's centre, the most charming children would get the extra plate of food, or the newest clothes.

Being highly compliant and agreeable is a strategy that they have learned is successful. They learn to be chameleons who adjust their views and behaviour to please whoever it is they feel they need to get on with that day.

◈ Given that the child will make themselves fit to different scenarios, they may not have a strong sense of self. If they use this approach for long enough, they may struggle to understand who they actually are, what they think, and what they like.

◈ One of the first things you should do is work hard with them to define who they are, what they like, and what their values are, in an age appropriate way. Working with a professional is recommended to support the work you do at home: it is our experience that kids with this attachment pattern have been in care for longer, or have suffered neglect or abuse.

◈ Issues with self-esteem are often challenging for these kids. Starting as early as possible to build a child's self-esteem is critical. Children like this are motivated by other people liking them, rather than any internal sense of worth. Seeking validation from other people is fraught with problems, more and more so as they get older. We'll often use phrases like, "Not everyone will like me, and I'm OK with that." We'll tell stories of when we adults have acted in a way that we believed was right, but it wasn't taken well by another person, and how that is OK.

◈ You need to rewire your child's brain to understand that they should first and foremost be true to their values, even if it doesn't suit another person. Work with them to create their value structure, speak regularly around their beliefs in simple language ("Anna believes in always telling the truth," for example), and discuss how things go when they apply this values-first approach.

◈ Teach your child to say NO. Without this skill, your child will become a target for bullies, and be open to abuse and risky situations. They will often be so polite and eager to keep random strangers happy that they will go along with situations that other children would run a mile from.

◈ In the case of children who are attaching easily to any adult, work with the adults in their life to get them to back off. Most adults will find it charming that they have a "special bond" and won't realise that it's fairly widespread and not helpful to the family dynamic.

◈ Create and reinforce the notion of family with photos, drawings, and well-chosen language. Carve out the idea for the child that this is a special unit that sits apart from the rest of the world.

◈ Find ways to teach loyalty to your child – loyalty to the family unit above all other things. Encourage them not to move through various friendships at a fast pace. Explain that maybe at preschool, when they're playing with someone, they keep playing with them for a while, and if someone else comes along who they'd like to play with, invite the other person to play, too.

◈ Encourage your child to play with the children, not the adults. This will be a long battle, but kick them outside with the kids, otherwise kids who attach easily to adults will sit up with a cup of tea and chat with the adults like that's absolutely normal.

◈ Model friendships yourself. This might take some time to rub off, but certainly in our lives, our children have seen the same small circle of family and close friends regularly through the years. We make a new friend here and there, but our longest friendships are so deep that they feel familial.

◈ You should assume that children who have spent longer stints in care will have attachment issues, whether you can see them or not. For children who have spent years in care, we strongly suggest you start regular counselling around attachment, self-esteem, making and keeping friends, and so on, right from the start. We did much of this at home, but should have seen that our boy needed more pre-emptive support.

◈ As children grow older, do not be afraid to parent them strongly. Our kids will go through long periods (months or years) with no phone, no social media, and under strict supervision. This ebbs and flows depending on where they are at, but we provide structure for them and try to prevent them from getting into situations where they can only fail. It's not foolproof and it's hard, high-energy parenting.

My Kid Is an Asshole: Angry, Controlling Children

Adoption is a funny thing: one minute your child is living in an institution, and the next they are yours. You fall in love with a child's photo, the image you create of your child in your mind. Sometimes they come home and they're all of that and more. And sometimes they come home and they are harder to love.

While we all get romantic about our new child, it's unrealistic to expect to fall head over heels in love with every child instantly. The older the child and the longer they have been institutionalised, the harder this early bonding will be. Adoptive parents who behave in a loving way will usually develop a strong attachment to their child, but what can vary enormously is how long it takes for the child to accept and then return this love.

We also tend to observe a higher-than-normal incidence of asshole tendencies amongst kids who were adopted. Professionals might call it oppositional defiance disorder. We might call it a deep-seated desire for control. All of it makes absolute sense, but parenting an oppositional adopted child can be hell.

These children have learned that some adults can't be trusted and that they need to control what happens to them in order to feel safe. In fact, paradoxically, it's when things are going well in the family that they tend to feel the least safe. Feelings of joy, happiness and love are too big to deal with and too threatening to submit to, so the child decides that it is better to go back to not engaging in order to feel in control. In doing so, they often blow up the relationship with the parent. Again and again. All makes sense, right? But translate that to a parent/child relationship, and you get a power struggle that takes years to overcome.

Early on, it can be hard to recognise that power struggle. It simply looks like bad behaviour that is frustrating and hard to parent. Let's give some examples of the power struggles you might face:

◇ A child who shouts all the time, who interrupts you and anyone else constantly, who talks incessantly and doesn't care that others might like to speak. I call it "taking up all of the airtime" of a family. Sometimes the only relief you get is when they are asleep. This behaviour is incredibly draining and in my experience, it makes me feel like I don't have a spare brain cell to think, because my head is so filled with this child's noise.

◇ A child who is happy when they have upset you. Often, this happens when they've had a nice time; maybe it's Christmas morning and they've received lovely gifts. You look across at them with such love, enjoying this wonderful moment. You might ask them which present was their favourite. They'll respond that they didn't really get much, or something similarly inflammatory.

◇ A child who has no ability to be flexible, who sulks or screams when plans change or things don't go their way. Perhaps you've told the child that the next day you'll go to the park. Come the next day, one of the other children is sick and you need to change your plans. While you explain all of this to the child, empathy isn't a strong point and they proceed to ruin everyone's day – in a sense to pay you back for ruining *their* day.

◈ A child who stands over their younger siblings, telling them to get dressed. When they don't move fast enough, they shout at them to hurry up!

◈ A child who will watch random families out and about and provide feedback: "I think your baby is hungry. I think your baby is cold." This comes across as cute and endearing in a small child; less so in a pre-teen.

◈ A child so frustrated by the lack of control she'd had over her life that she would use snot and spit as a weapon, or simply stand and pee in the middle of her room. When she was unhappy with something, she would stand and force snot to run out from her nose. Then, she would let spit from her mouth leak out and pool at her feet. She would groan and stay this way for ages. It didn't matter where we were, and in fact she realised it was far more effective in public.

◈ A child who behaves badly most of the time. You work so hard to remain peaceful and calm in your guidance of them; then that one time you raise your voice, or react angrily, they behave like a wounded animal and continue to bring up how mean and awful you are. This happened to me recently. My son was being a major pain in the ass; I did my usual calm, rational explanation, my composed application of consequences, my deep breathing, then suggested he go outside to skateboard. When he turned his back, I stuck up my middle finger at him. Show me a parent who isn't immature like that from time to time! Trouble was, he turned around as I did it. He refused my apology, repeating how wrong it was for a mother to give her child the "rude finger". All this from a child who had lied to me, stolen from me, and not listened to me so many times. I screw up once, and it's etched into his memory for life!

Parenting an oppositional child is one of the hardest things I've ever done. Most days I would wake up serene and peaceful, ready to be a calm and understanding parent. Then my son would walk in and I would go from Dalai-Lama calm to full of anger, all within our first couple of minutes of interaction.

◆   ◆   ◆

Here are some tips for parenting a controlling child:

◊   First and foremost, put yourself in their shoes and have empathy for how out of control life must feel or have felt for them. Accept that their need for control is a mechanism they use to feel safe, rather than a deliberate attempt to upset everyone around them.

◊   Use the "I Wonder" technique that we explain in the Therapy Toolbox section. Something like, "I wonder if you need everything to be just like you want it because you haven't been able to choose much in your life?" Describing a behaviour and its associated feelings in an age appropriate way takes some of the sting out of it. It equips your child with the words and tools they need to try to understand themselves, which, in time, is likely to lead to some improvement in this behaviour.

◊   Wherever you can, give your child a choice between two things. Let them feel some control when it's safe to do so, but limit the choices.

◊   When you are at an impasse with an angry child, try the healing power of "Dad jokes" or farts (or, even better, Dad jokes about farts). Sometimes, no matter what you do or try, your child will get angry and you will find yourself in conflict, and nothing will reach them. You can't reason with them – quite literally, because they cannot access their pre-frontal cortex, which is the seat of higher learning and circumspection, and they are stuck in an emotional state. What you need is something that cuts through the seriousness of the situation and breaks the circuit of anger. Depending on the age of the child, you may wish to try a silent-but-deadly fart whilst holding a serious face and saying something like, "How do you like my new perfume?" Often, I've found that the child is looking for some way out of their situation but can't find one, and allowing them to go on about how disgusting you are is a release (pun intended) for them. Extra points if your farts make a funny noise – all kids struggle not to laugh at a funny fart noise. You can also try out your repertoire of lame Dad jokes that are truly cringe-worthy. In short, any silly, non-serious behaviour is worth a try. Dad dancing is also recommended.

◈ Where you can't let your child choose, use words to explain your role as parent. Tell them that sometimes, parents have to choose for their children to keep them safe, and that this is all part of loving their child. Tell them that you appreciate it can be hard when you can't decide for yourself, and that you understand that.

◈ Work on their ability to be flexible. When plans have to change, explain why and acknowledge that you understand it's hard for them when things change. Allow them to feel let down or disappointed. Praise them for recovering when they do.

◈ Promote and emphasise your role as a parent who will keep them safe. Creating this trust in them will reduce controlling behaviour over time – but it can take a long, long time.

◈ Try not to take things personally. Again, this is hard, but it's not really about you – the behaviour is driven by your child's life experience.

◈ Pre-empt a likely blow-up by saying something like, "Hey, you know, we have had a great day together, it has been really fun. Remember that sometimes after a great day, you find something to get upset about and get angry. Well, we need to keep an eye out for that – what do you think?" And if something does happen, you can say dispassionately, "Hey, we thought something might happen, and there it is." This helps your child to recognise their behaviour and gives them something to think about for next time, building self-awareness and ultimately self-control.

Post-Traumatic Stress Disorder

One of our kids had severe Post-Traumatic Stress Disorder (PTSD). We'd never dealt with it before, known anyone suffering from it, or had any idea of the wide-ranging impact PTSD could have on someone. PTSD is generally the result of a single traumatic event, like a car crash or the loss of a parent, that overwhelms a person's ability to cope. Imagine how hard it must be to have PTSD compounded with trauma at a developmental stage as a child.

It took a while to manifest, with the first few months of living together requiring a lot of adjustment. It was frustrating at times, but otherwise uneventful. We were bonding, getting to know each other's likes and dislikes, and making sure that our children's clothes and rooms were how they wanted them. Our affected child was much older, and the early days of living together were akin to having a visitor in your home that you're trying to keep happy.

That "visitor" feeling wore off for our girl a few months in, and she started to get really argumentative with us. Every meal, outing, or interaction with someone was slightly stressful as she was highly unpredictable, and it was hard to control her behaviour. She would deliberately disrupt family meals to get everyone else feeling as angry as she was. It was early days in our adoptive parenting journey, so we used to feel some embarrassment about her behaviour. She would moan or scream, and didn't care at all if people looked at her strangely.

When a child is hell-bent on making you angry, you may start out patient and calm but, until you are skilled with this dynamic, it is hard to avoid getting mad after being provoked and provoked and provoked.

Our child had been provoking us for a response for weeks. We went on holidays with extended family, and it was the first time most of them had met our two new children. Her behaviour had me on high alert, and I had an uneasy feeling in my stomach just from her being around. Getting her to sit and eat with everyone at the table was a drama; getting her to speak nicely was a drama; getting her to agree to whatever outing we all had planned was impossible; and getting her to bed at a decent hour (and you'll understand, all we wanted to do was to get her to bed so we could have a break) was a shouting match every night. It was all made a little worse because we weren't in the privacy of our home.

It was our last night before we were to fly home. She had been misbehaving all day, so we calmly took her into her bedroom and sat with her and told her she needed to stay in here with us for a little while. This enraged her, and we saw her first violent outburst. We were totally unprepared. She lurched at me and grabbed both of my nipples, twisting them; then she went for my arms and hands, and began hitting out at both of us as we pulled her hands off me. Her eyes were vacant: she was absolutely unreachable. Inexperienced as we were with this kind of behaviour, we spoke with her, tried to reason with her, shouted at her. It was futile to talk; she was so far away. Seeing someone flip like this was frightening – like when you see someone "possessed" in a movie. We had no idea what to do, and this confrontation ended with us sitting on the floor gently restraining her so she would stop hitting and punching at me, until she calmed down.

We then had to go out and face our family and try to brush off the issue – they'd heard her screams as she'd been going for a couple of hours, and they'd been watching the other kids.

This was the first of many violent outbursts in our house. It lasted the best part of a year, though it felt much longer, so deeply did it affect our relationship and our parenting. Her anger was focused at me as the mother, and it was frightening at times as she was strong, angry and close to my size. We could tell when violence was brewing, as she would agitate us for a few hours and keep escalating until we were mad and would seek to remove her. Then, she would start hitting, kicking, hair-pulling. The best strategy when this was happening was to remove the other kids, and for me to stay away from her. My husband would sit with her, often restraining her, for hours, caught between her anger and mine. That might surprise you – that I was angry, too. But it's impossible not to be when someone goads you and wrecks day after day and event after event for your family, and then lunges at you to hit you.

We were getting some help with this child, but things continued to escalate on a daily basis until one day, we had to load her into the car, restrained by three adults as she tried to hit me in the front seat and grab the steering wheel from her father. We took her to her psychiatrist for emergency treatment. She was disassociated, and he was better able to treat her having seen the extent of her rage – when she wasn't in this state, she was timid around people, and he didn't take our claims of her behaviour seriously.

In the car, Robbie Williams' "Angels" was playing on the radio as she screamed and lunged and screamed and lunged at us. Hearing it now takes me straight back to that day when I felt like our newly created family was cursed and that life was over for us. Parenting someone with PTSD is immensely difficult. Their mental state is so anguished that it can destroy the rest of the family. It can make you think about turning the wheel just a little to the left on your drive home so you can escape this life. Really.

◆　◆　◆

The cycle of anger, provocation, violence, restraint and then calm is a volatile one. Understanding what is happening, keeping your child and your family safe, and getting professional help, are all key. We didn't really appreciate the extent to which our daughter was suffering from PTSD; I don't remember it coming up in our adoption counselling, and it wasn't an illness either of us had witnessed before. I wish I had known more about it at the start, because understanding makes any difficulty a little easier.

Some lessons we've learned:

◈ Don't discount PTSD as the cause of your child's issues. You don't need to have experienced war to have PTSD – the loss of a birth family can absolutely lead to PTSD. Get professional help.

◈ Medication may make the world of difference. We were defiantly anti-medication before we had our daughter. We have since done an about-face on this issue, as we've seen the way that medication can take some of the edge off for our kids and allow the family a little respite during very traumatic times. It is important that you not only have a plan for putting the child on the medication, but also for taking them off it. Medication rarely makes the underlying issues go away, but it can give the child some breathing space to work on things.

◈ Counselling, with a counsellor experienced in trauma, is vital. Commit to this as part of the fabric of your family – vary the frequency, but don't drop the ball when the hard times pass.

◈ PTSD can destroy a family as it manifests with violence, dysfunctional relationships and anti-social behaviours. Initially, if our daughter was having an episode or gearing up for one, we would cancel whatever plans we had as a family. But we soon realised that we couldn't *all* be driven by her PTSD. Instead, we stopped taking our daughter out to places that might be difficult. Try to find ways to still interact with the world as a family – can one of you stay home with your PTSD child while the other takes the rest of the family out? Is there a place where your PTSD child tends to fare OK? Find more time to do that as a family.

◈ When you're in the middle of an episode, and you're parenting as a couple, it may be necessary to have both of you on hand. If you have other children, try to arrange with a friend or neighbour to remove the other children for a little while. While we had a violent child, it was never directed at the other children. Our advice to remove them is simply so they don't have to see the rages and the necessary restraint. Our kids say they don't remember much of this; they were too small. I wish we had been able to better deal with this dynamic and remove them.

◈ If you live close to other people, you might want to speak to your neighbours about what your family is going through. When our daughter was violent, she would often scream, "They're trying to kill me!" I lived in fear of the local police turning up.

◈ Believe that things can get better. Our child who had PTSD is now functioning well. She hasn't had an episode for many years, and our relationships are repaired. Any pain we felt – me especially, for being the regular target of her violence – is forgiven. In the midst of our bad year or two, I truly believed we had ruined the lives of everyone in our family and that we would never get past this situation. I fantasised about how I could remove this child from our home or, failing that, about how I could leave my husband so I didn't have to live with her. This sounds ridiculously over-the-top as I write it, but these were truly my feelings at the time. If you are feeling hopeless and depressed, that's a really normal reaction.

◈ Take it easy on yourself. Parenting a child with PTSD takes every ounce of calm you possess, and some days, you won't be the best parent ever. Just do your best. Try to get a break from this child, especially an overnight break where you can sleep easy and not be stressed about what might happen. I remember the couple of times that our daughter had a sleepover with a friend's family who we knew well. In all of my life, I can't remember ever feeling as free as I did when we dropped her off, knowing we were getting a break for 24 hours.

◈ Forgive. While you rationally understand this was never about you, it's only human to feel hurt and resentful when you have bore the brunt of these behaviours. It's made worse by the frustration you feel that you're trying to provide a safe and loving family for the child: "I'm trying to *help* her!"

Every Man for Himself and Creating Sibling Bonds

Recently, I was chatting with our kids, who knew we were writing a book about adoptive parenting, and I asked what advice they would give other adoptive families. One of them suggested that it was a good idea to adopt more than one child, so that they each had someone like them, a "brother in arms".

This surprised me. Not because it's a strange concept: to me, it's totally logical and sensible. It surprised me because with my adopted children, their sibling interactions often resemble *Lord of the Flies* or, at the very least, every child for themselves.

Of course, this is not universally true; there are times when they'll generously share a treat with a sibling. But it *is* true a lot more often than I expected it would be. Some days I wonder if they would kill each other, if I didn't intervene.

I thought our adopted kids would see each other as comrades, each born in a world far different to here, and in similar circumstances. But instead, they see each other as competition. I know, I know, all kids do this with their siblings – but it is far more extreme with our adopted children.

The kids are kind and giving to others who are close to us: little cousins, neighbours, friends. But the same courtesy is not extended within our house, where siblings are competitors – for parental attention, for positive or negative feedback, for the sofa they like to lie on, to hold their favourite pet, to eat the last bit of the food.

Initially we believed it was simply lack of awareness, that they were off in their own little worlds, doing their own thing, without a great deal of thought to anyone else. But I have since learned how wrong this belief is: they *are* watching. Not only are they watching, they are counting, tallying and comparing, and if they sense they've come out short, they'll act on it.

One of our kids had a history of troubled behaviour at school, which we worked hard on for years. Eventually, with consistent discipline, love, therapy and, I believe, increased maturity on his part, he came through it. We were delighted, and could let our guard down a bit with him.

Meanwhile, one of the other kids was having a hard time, the first serious bumps since her adoption, and it was pretty serious. This child was getting most of our parenting attention over and above the basics of feed/clothe/school. We knew our boy had enough awareness to see his sibling was struggling, and he was quite generous in giving us the space we needed to chat about complex issues and work with our other child. He would play with the younger kids to try and look after them. We thought he really got it and was helping, and we were really proud of how empathetic and kind he had become.

Then he started to complain about hating his teacher at school. This continued day in, day out. The teacher started complaining about him, and we were back on the well-trodden road of calls from school and low-level misbehaviour. We recovered fairly swiftly from our annoyance at being back at the stage of our stomachs tightening every time the phone rang, and tried to work with him to figure it out.

It turned out he was jealous of the all the attention mum and dad were giving his sibling. Instead of telling us this, he started misbehaving. When our family therapist asked him what was going on (after many hours of my husband and I hypothesising about potential causes and missing this one that was *staring us in the face*), he opened up easily, and it was simple: *You spend all your time with my sister, you only want to hear what she has to say, you only worry about her, she is getting taken to lots of appointments and gets donuts afterwards, we get dragged around with her, I have to play with my little sibling because she's missing out too, you let my sister sleep in bed with mum and you never let me.* And so on.

It was all legitimate and fair – we *had* done that. We thought at some level, the kids understood; he'd had a good few years where most of our parental energy was expended on him. It tends to go in cycles.

We didn't want to go into detail about what was happening with his sister, but we did try to seek his understanding, acceptance and help on the big picture concept of looking after each other. He agreed to that, but it was only after hearing it in adult, persuasive words.

We also tried to make more of an effort to spend better time with the other kids, making sure they felt heard and loved, and thanking them when they were supportive of the broader family.

Another occasion I can think of was when two of the kids were at a school event and one of them won a prize: money to spend on a treat at the canteen. He bought something for himself and another child. I expected that he would have shared this with his sibling, instead of a child he'd just met.

On another occasion, at a school disco, he was tasked with picking a team, and he simply would not pick his sister. Instead, he left her hanging for many rounds, which really upset me. We spoke about it afterwards and said it was us against the world – we look after each other first, before friends and before anyone else.

But still, after a decade, for the kids it's more "every man for himself" than "taking care of our own". This makes sense, given their attachment with us is still changing, and hasn't always been secure. Anyone else distracting us from them must seem very threatening.

We still work on it, to this day. When my time is done, I want to leave the world knowing we've built an unusual family, but one that supports and loves each other without question. It's a work in progress.

◆　◆　◆

Here are some tips for boosting the sense of family:

◈   As a family, we model generous giving. If we make a cup of tea, we'll ask everyone else who'd like one, and not moan when people accept. We make sure there's plenty of food, always enough for seconds. We want as few reasons as possible for competition amongst siblings.

◈   We now have no doubt that the kids notice when one child is getting a lot of attention. Even if they logically understand, they store it all up and either misbehave or get resentful. Even though your energy might be depleted when there are issues with another child, taking a couple of hours to do something one-on-one with the other children will reduce the chance of a domino effect of misbehaviour. Even if you don't have any current issues in the family, you'll stave things off if you can take an hour now and then to have some one-on-one time with each of your children. They'll talk to you in a much more meaningful way than when they are fighting for airtime with others.

◈   Talk a lot about your family unit: in our family, we do X, and we do Y. Even use phrases that sound a bit trite to you: "In the Jones' household, family always comes first and we look after each other before anyone else."

◈   Try to find games and activities that you can do as a family. We love Uno (it's accompanied us on many holidays and dinners out), or a pack of playing cards for "Jacks, Twos and Eights" and Bananagrams. The kids also like Trouble, though it makes me a bit crazy.

◈   After a recent holiday, where we spent intensive amounts of time together doing fun things, we're making an effort to have family days out now and again. We generally try not to overschedule weekends as we have very busy weeks, and while everyone moans about it a bit, getting up a bit earlier, packing some towels and swimmers and bags of chips and going for a hike and a swim is a great way to bond and shut out the world for a while.

◈ Show this sense of family as much as you talk about it. Display family photos around the house (embarrassingly, we took years to do this properly). Speak about and celebrate what you love about each other. Build each other up, and show the kids how to do this.

◈ Compliment the kids when they're kind to each other – or at least not trying to attack each other.

◈ When kids have a fractious relationship, it can be the path of least resistance to separate them – never letting them sit next to each other in the car, for example. We did this with some of our kids as we want a quiet life, but I think we made a mistake and should have forced them together so they could learn to get along.

◈ A topic of conversation we've recently introduced to the dinner table, to try to stem selfishness, is to go around answering the question, "What did you do for someone else today?" This is a new technique, but if we keep it going, I know it will cement the thought in the kids' minds. It also gives us a chance to praise them for being good to others. Let's hope it rubs off on how they treat their siblings.

◈ All three of us feel that if you can, you should adopt more than one child. We believe wholeheartedly that your adopted child will feel far less "weird" with someone else like them.

Rejection: You're Not My Real Mother

When you're an adoptive parent, you'll be overwhelmed with people telling you they've considered adoption, or longed to adopt or foster. Far less frequently, you'll have a longer conversation with someone who is genuinely considering becoming an adoptive parent. These are refreshing conversations, because they move from the "You're so good" vibe to an open and real conversation.

It's difficult to provide a balanced view "from the trenches", so to speak; it depends on what day it is and how things are on the home front. If it's been calm and lovely, as is often the case, they'll hear about how wonderful it is, with a sprinkling of challenges they should be ready for. If you've been at the kids' school back and forth all week for low-level misbehaviour and you just caught your child taking a $20 note out of your wallet, they're likely to get quite a different balance of the good, the bad and the ugly.

It's interesting to hear the worries and issues on the minds of potential adoptive parents. One of the key ones I hear is the pre-emptive sadness that their child will one day say to them, "You're not my real mother!"

Once you've been adoptive or foster parenting for a while, you will have heard this multiple times. My advice is to relax: it's just not about you.

If you were raised by your biological family, I bet you shouted at your parents, at least once in your hormone-fuelled teenage years, "I wish you weren't my parents!" This phrase is a weapon designed to wound, as is "You're not my real mother." It is said on the spur of the moment to someone who is loved, to express sadness, frustration, guilt and/or disappointment.

I've been hearing it now and again since my kids were preschoolers. When they were small, it was in response to a limitation imposed on them. It was in the vein of: my real mother would let me do this. I found the best response to this was to hug them, stay calm and unemotional, and soothe them with words. I'd say something like, "I know you miss your birth mother. It's OK to miss your birth mother. I'm sorry you don't get to live with her. I won't let you walk next to the road without holding my hand because I love you and need to keep you safe."

By the time I'd said all of that and dispensed a cuddle, the outburst was forgotten and we'd moved on. I never took this sentiment on personally; I let these comments wash over me and accepted them as normal.

What I would try to do, though, is start speaking with the kids, perhaps later that day, about what families were. I'd explain to them that they had two families: a birth mum who they would look like, who they would have lots of things in common with – maybe the same laugh or liking the same foods – and whose tummy they had grown in, but who (for whatever reason applies to the child) was not able to look after them. While the children were younger, before they understood how conception works, I found it simpler and sufficient to focus on the birth mother. They would not have any questions about the birth father just yet.

I would then explain that they also had our family. We had gone to court and told the judge that, yes, we loved this child and promised to look after them forever. We'd talk about what made a family: living together, loving each other, eating meals together, making sure the children go to school and have clothes and enough to eat, and always, *always* caring about each other and having one another in our lives. I'd usually add that, for me, that was what a "real" family was, if people ever wanted to argue about what "real" meant.

We'd follow that approach time and again, and the children grew to understand this language and use it themselves comfortably. Of course, they'd still lob "You're not my real mum" at me now and then, but they knew the last thing they'd do was upset me; instead, we'd have the usual conversation again.

The rejection of family changes in tone as the kids get older and their comprehension is expanded. It's still a little about boundaries, but a lot more about fantasy. You might be arguing with your child about whether they can do something they really want to do – let's say, play a particular sport – that for whatever reason you won't allow them to. They'll accept it for the day, and then come back and argue again. And again the next day, and the next day. You'll start to show a bit of frustration at being badgered, and they'll start to get mad – really mad. Soon enough, it will blow up. And it will blow up monumentally.

Your child will rail and moan and whine, and say how unfair and mean you are, how you are trying to ruin their life and that you won't let them do *anything*. Usually what follows is them asking when can they move out, and a statement that they're going back to their birth country or town where people love them. Let's just say that after days of the same to-and-fro, and with the knowledge of an impending eruption, you're going to be pretty over the whole conversation by then.

You would not be the first parent to retort: "I don't want you to, but if you have to go, then go." I've done it, and my friends have done it. But we try really hard not to, and I encourage you to resist the temptation as well.

There are two reasons for this: on several occasions, the kids have taken our frustrated response literally and ran off. This prompts a manhunt and a whole lot of angst and worry.

The second reason is that's what the kids want you to say, so they can justify feeling angry and hurt by you. You've done all this work; just try your very best to hold off and let them cool down.

◆　◆　◆

Here are some ideas for surviving the rejection of your family and idealisation of the birth family:

◊ Use language around families correctly. In our house, we use "birth" or "biological" family, and *our* family. We don't say "adoptive family" or "real family". If someone asks me if a child is my "real" baby, I'll say she is my biological child. Sometimes I might throw in, "They are all my real babies!" That tends to fluster people, though.

◊ Be as open as you can with your children about what you know of the reasons why they are not with their birth families. Try not to romanticise it or speculate to fill in gaps. We do say we are sure that their birth parents loved them very much – because we *are* sure.

◊ Don't take the rejection of you or your family personally. It will happen a million times in this parenting journey, just as it would in a biological family. It just may feel a little more hurtful in an adoptive family. Toughen up on this one: laugh it off, shrug your shoulders, make a joke, or best of all, suggest to your child that they're angry and you should have this conversation later.

A Novel Approach to Attachment: Rebirthing

After parenting him for a few years, I thought my four-year-old understood what adoption meant. We'd always talked about picking him up from the children's centre and I had shown him photos, as well as photos of his birth family.

It wasn't until a close friend gave birth to her daughter that he really understood.

After visiting the baby in hospital, he asked where the baby came from. I explained that the baby had been in her belly ("Remember she had a big tummy?") and then she gave birth and now the baby was out.

He tried to link that to his story: "So I was in your tummy, then you pushed me out?" I explained that he had grown in his birth mother's tummy, and then we picked him up from the orphanage. "But my sisters and brother grew in your tummy?" Yes, I explained, "They grew in my tummy and it would have been nice if I got to have you in my tummy, too, but that would mean that you wouldn't be you. And you are perfect. You are you because you came from your birth parents, and that is wonderful."

"But I want to be in your tummy," he responded with real sadness. Usually, his dramatic displays of sadness don't lend themselves to sympathy. But this – his lip quivering, trying to hold back tears – was different. My heart hurt.

We hugged, we rocked, and I showered him with love that day. I talked to him about how it doesn't matter how families are formed, just that we are a family and we all love each other – all the time wishing his deep sadness would lift.

But this wise little boy developed a form of therapy to help him come to terms with his feelings about birth. The next day, he climbed up under my dress and asked me to give birth to him.

I obliged. I am a midwife and *love* pregnancy, birth and babies. I am also what some may call dramatic, so acting out labour and birth was great fun. I moaned and groaned and swayed and pushed, until this sweet baby boy was born. My daughters walked into the room at that very moment of birth. They saw what was happening and quickly joined in: "Oh, our little baby brother! He is so sweet!" The giant smile on his face was reward enough for our efforts. I swaddled him and rocked him. I kissed him a million times and told him I was so happy to have such a sweet baby boy.

He asked me to birth him several times a day for a couple of weeks. It then lessened to once a day, then once every few days, then stopped all together. Each time, he grinned with delight. It seems this "birth" was enough to reassure him that I am his mother. That he is my baby. And that we are a family.

I would never have suggested this strange approach to him. In fact, I would never even have thought of it. Speak openly with your children and sometimes they might lead you somewhere that seems strange, but is in fact *exactly* what they need.

When a Child Has No Information About Their Past

During the preparations to adopt, a lot of time is spent thinking about how you will speak to your children about their circumstances. You will have probably practised how you might explain to your child why they aren't with their birth parents. Some of you may have open adoptions, where there's less need for long explanations.

If you are adopting intercountry, you will probably have learned about that country and picked up some phrases from their language. You may even have bought art from the country and outfits for use at home, in an effort to create some ties to the life they have left behind.

In some cases, we can tell our children stories about why they were adopted, who their families were, and how much they were loved. We know their birth mother and father's names, what languages they spoke and, sometimes, what they looked like.

For some of our children though, we know almost nothing.

We don't know their given name. We don't know their family name, their parents, where they were born, whether they had brothers or sisters. We don't even know their birthday. Their stories are empty and it's hard not to feel heartbroken about this, especially when they contrast their scant backstory with the far richer stories of siblings or friends.

All we know is a few snippets from the people who took them into care. They are generally pretty sad snippets that you might not want a child to overly identify with as their backstory. These kids have usually been taken into care because of neglect, abandonment, illness or injury. They often suffer the double whammy of a very tough, unknown start to life; then, as they work through this and, like so many adopted children, seek the comfort of holding onto a feeling of who they are and the fact that they were loved, they discover that there is absolutely no satisfaction there for them.

◆   ◆   ◆

Sometimes, adoptive parents face many unanswerable questions that create a deep inner sadness in our children. We will never be able to answer these questions. There are gaps in our children's history, unknown medical records and unnamed birth families.

When the kids were still small and asked about their pasts, we were able to answer their questions simply. As they get older, we tend to seek to overcompensate where we can, collect physical memorabilia as we go along, tell stories and patch up those emotional wounds of "why or how" with whatever information we have – but it gets harder, much harder.

Sometimes we don't know what to say next. Imagine not knowing where it all started. Imagine not knowing where you get your long legs from, or your fantastic laugh. Was my birth mother beautiful? What did she look like? Was my birth father kind to her? Did I have any biological brothers and sisters? Do they think about me? Where was I found? Why was I there? How did I get there? Why was I injured? Why was I adopted and no one else was? What happened to the other children?

These questions make me feel like someone is stabbing me when I hear them. They make me want to get on a plane, march back into the place my child was found, and start screaming for someone tell me *something* so I can heal my little girl's pain. I think how unfair it is that my child has to live with these emotions swirling around her brain.

There is no magic solution and, pre-adoption, I was naïve. Hands up! I thought I could handle this. In fact, I will go as far as to say that I didn't give it a huge amount of thought. I may even have believed that having birth family information would be more difficult than having nothing, as I would then have all the answers when maybe I didn't want them. I was wrong! Having adopted two of my children under equally tough but hugely different circumstances, I can now assure you that having nothing is so much harder.

◆   ◆   ◆

A recent conversation around the table at lunchtime brought up some of these issues. All four children were there, and my husband began to shift in his seat at the questions and made pleas with his eyes for me to answer, as he simply didn't know what to say. Neither did I.

We sat and listened to her voice cracking with emotion and sadness. Her four-year-old sister started to stroke her arm. She could see her sadness, but didn't understand why. She will never feel this same pain that her sister has; she doesn't have these unanswered questions. She knows where it all began. I am her birth mother. She is only four, and yet she is at peace with her biological heritage because we are here to tell the tales. Tears rolled down my cheeks as I struggled to find the right thing to say.

We spoke at length about her birth country and how she would feel about going back to visit. She couldn't control her feelings of sadness, and started sobbing. She is scared of the unknown, the "what ifs", and yet she is so desperate to go and see the children's centre, to meet those who cared for her, to see the room where she slept, to see the airport, to walk the streets, to experience her roots.

It all came out: "People ask me at school why I was adopted, and I don't know why." Major, epic parenting fail. Why wasn't she armed with a response? We'd talked about this so much; I thought she had it down pat! As she told us what had been said at school, the ignorance of some of her classmates, their parents and the teachers made me want to march to school and set everybody straight the very next morning.

◆ ◆ ◆

Here are some ideas for dealing with a child who knows little about
their past:

◇ Firstly, always tell the truth and try not to pad out what you know
   with illusion. At the same time, though, don't avoid trying to
   provide them with a better sense of identity.

◇ Seek out links for them. When they laugh, for example, you could
   wonder if they got their laugh from their birth mother or father.
   Talk about where they are from, what it was like, what life was like
   for people living there. Engage with your child on the things they
   wonder about: "Do you wonder what your birth mother looked
   like? I'll bet she was tall and beautiful." Or, "I think your birth
   father was good at running, like you!" Never make wondering
   about their birth family off limits – don't overdo it, but I think
   it comforts the child to know you think about their other family
   from time to time, that you also wonder about their origins.

◇ Allow them to fantasise. They will probably create a god-like
   image of their birth parents in their mind and there's nothing to
   be gained from reality-checking a child who will never know their
   people. Let them dream.

◇ Overcompensate. As soon as you are the parent of this child,
   you need to make up for lost time and build a history from that
   moment. Photos, stories and memories are vital. If you are missing
   large chunks, you need to work harder to create a sense of self in
   your child.

◇ Highlight any familial connections that you do have within the
   adopted family. You might not know where your child got her long
   legs from, but you do know that you and she laugh at the same
   jokes and like the same movies.

◇ We have found that, in our family, the child who knows little has
   taken on the birth family of the child who knows more. She knows,
   at an intellectual level, that they are not hers, but she has taken
   them on anyway. We all allow that; I can't see it doing much harm.

◈ It's OK that you sometimes don't know what to say. It's OK to simply be sad with them. Compassion, empathy and understanding are key, rather than reassurance. You do not know how this feels for them. Phrases like, "This must be so hard for you" are far more powerful than, "I know you're sad. I get sad sometimes." Don't belittle their sadness.

◈ I try not to let on that it makes me deeply sad that I can't tell my child when they were born, or what name was chosen for them.

The Odd One Out: Part 1

We had two biological girls when we started our adoption journey. We had hoped to be able to adopt twins, or two children at the same time. Unfortunately, the country we were adopting from would not allow us to have more than three children in total. We assured them that we were both financially and physically able to care for more than three children, but due to government policies, we were denied two children.

So, our family ended up being made of three biological children and one adopted child – not what we had planned, but wonderful nonetheless. Our adopted son slotted right into the sibling group and is truly adored (and annoyed) by his siblings. They have a wonderful "team" mentality which I think was encouraged by us moving between different countries a few times in their early years. We always holiday together as a family, and they often only have each other for company. I take millions of photos of the four of them, and have them proudly displayed around the house. The two boys share a room (and clothes, as they are the same size). For the most part, it doesn't even factor that our son was adopted.

That is, according to the rest of us – his parents and his siblings.

For him, however, it is a constant struggle to believe that he belongs in this family.

When I asked him directly about how he feels about being adopted, he said, "It's weird." He tells me that even though he likes being in this family, it feels strange that the others came from my tummy and he didn't. He doesn't like the fact that he was adopted, and he doesn't like that people ask questions about it, reminding him that he is different. Looking different is enough to make other people notice and ask questions, but feeling different inside is what he finds the hardest. He finds it difficult because even though we feel like home to him, there is a part of him that feels like he belongs somewhere else. He says he feels a longing to connect with his birth family and to know how they feel about him. All of this is totally understandable, but it is painful for us to hear these things from our son. We hate that he doesn't feel 100% content, but we can't do anything to take away that deep longing for his birth family or to truly instil that feeling of completely belonging and never questioning your place in the family.

I think it is unfair for him to be the odd one out in our family. In some ways, he feels extra special – he gets both a birthday and an adoption day celebration. We all make a big fuss over him, and the other kids say it is not fair that he gets two special days (his siblings' jealousy makes him so satisfied!). We often have long, cuddly talks about his birth country and his birth family. These conversations bond us together, and his brother feels a little left out in these moments. However, I know that the other three children feel very secure within themselves, and that this son doesn't. Allowing him to feel that bit special, and for him to see them envious, is great for his sense of self-worth.

I think it would be a lot easier for him if he had a sibling who was also adopted, so they could feel similar within the family, but at times I think he enjoys the fact that he has a country besides Australia that is special and particular to him (just like his father does with Greece). We try our best to drill into our children that their role as siblings is to take care of each other. I am so proud when they are not fighting and take the time to help one another, when the girls piggy-back the boys or help them with their reading, or when the boys work together to build a fort. It brings us so much joy to see our children demonstrate so clearly the meaning of family, no matter how we became one.

We are lucky to have close friends with adopted children and try to spend as much time with them as possible. His best friend in the world was also adopted, and they share a special bond. I think they find comfort in the fact that their lives have been so similar, and they don't have to explain anything to the other person.

The Odd One Out:
Part 2

Families that blend biological and adoptive children are beautiful things. All three of us have them, and we all wondered how things would work – and we can assure you, it does.

One of our families is made up of three adopted children and one biological child. Many people wonder aloud if they could love "another person's child" as much as "their own". If you've read this far, you'll understand that these are not phrases we use, or a worldview we subscribe to. But with absolute assurance we can tell you that, yes, you do love your adopted children as much as your biological children. In fact, often your feelings for your adopted children are perhaps more raw, as you go through more together, and you may also overlay your feelings about their earlier lives in your approach to them. You almost feel your biological child has had it easy compared to the other children. I have once or twice said to my biological child in exasperation: "You are meant to be the easy one!"

One of the saddest aspects of parenting adopted and biological children is the real or imagined contrasts between the formative years of their infancies. I've seen how our baby was showered with love, attention and stimulation from the moment we knew she existed in utero. I think about my adopted children and the trauma of separation they must have felt. I think of them being confused and sad and desperately missing their birth families the day they went into care, with no understanding of what was happening. I think of them sitting in an institution with carers who looked after them, but who didn't love them as their own. I think of them fighting with other kids for the bigger plate of food, a chance to play with the ball, a hug from a carer. I think about them fending for themselves, fighting for themselves, the cuts and scrapes that were just part of institutional life.

I remember saying to one of my adopted children years ago, "You need *so* many hugs! Why do you need so many hugs?" She didn't skip a beat as she said it was because no one had hugged her in the centre. My heart still hurts a little every time I recall that story – because that had been her reality, and because I had felt suffocated to the point where I would even ask that.

Early on, I was sensitive to the feelings of our adopted kids when it came to this biological baby. From the start, she was *our* baby collectively, particularly as we hadn't really planned on having babies and were begged by our other kids to have her. They felt a sense of ownership of her from the start. We played them a DVD of her in utero and somewhere, on some decommissioned laptop, I have videos of them squealing with delight as they watched. In fact, rather than creating a biological divide, it glued us together more securely as a family; it was something we were all part of.

I was also careful of the way I spoke to her about growing in my tummy if the other kids were around, or when people remarked that she looked like me or my husband after she was born. My caution has reduced over time, as we've realised the kids just aren't that sensitive to this. I think that means we're doing OK in making them all feel as loved as each other. In fact, the kids themselves often laugh that my biological daughter runs like me, and has my bum. And she is certainly as pedantic and precise as her father!

We often muse about how interesting our biological child's life will be: how the family she's grown up with is such a different construct to all of those around her. What will it be like for her to be the only white child? Will she feel jealous of the intense parenting and learning support the other children often get? Will she feel that we have different or higher expectations of her?

The only thing that bothers her right now is that the other kids get a family day on or around the day they were adopted. No presents, just cake. She doesn't understand why she shouldn't have a family day, too. We started to let her piggyback on our eldest's family day. No big deal.

Right now, it's hard to tell what it's like for her to be the odd one out. Our baby is in her early years of school, and her understanding of adoption is growing by the day. She has always known her siblings were born in Africa. At times, she may have thought she was African, too – in preschool, she liked going to International Day in her big sister's West African batik dress and beaded necklace.

She has started to ask more complex questions, though. When she was annoyed with a sibling, for example, she asked if we could send them back! She has asked some strange questions, like whether you can buy a child. Currently, her most consistent line of questioning is about herself and where she fits in, rather than about the other kids. Our family existed for almost four years before she came along, so we often speak about holidays or events pre-her, and she spends her time trying to figure out if she was born yet.

I expect, based on the journeys I've observed with the other kids, that her line of enquiry will move towards "why". Why did we adopt the kids? What is the story with their birth family? And we will give her honest and age-appropriate responses to these questions.

There is occasionally some jealousy from the other kids towards her. It seems less driven by her being biologically ours, and more to do with the attention she gets from being youngest. When she was a baby, they were sensitive to the amount of attention they were getting. Was this worse than in any family adjusting to a new arrival? Probably not.

There can also be some jealousy from the other kids because she is a compliant child who finds school easy. She brings home award after award from school. The kids feel the contrast between "Miss Perfect" and themselves. We try hard not to differentiate between them in this way, and celebrate the kids' individual strengths (refer to

"Accepting the Children You Have" in the Parental Self-Care section). Academic success is not the hallmark of achievement for us in the way that it is for so many professional families; that would only lead to pain for all of us. Both my husband and I were among the first to be university-educated in our families, and we were very hardworking academically. Of course, it gives us pleasure when a child of ours is good at school – saying anything else would be disingenuous. But I get that same pleasure and excitement from seeing my son build complex Lego structures, or reading a song my daughter has written.

When a Birth Parent Dies

We'd always wanted our daughter to feel connected to her birthplace and its culture. We did the usual things, like buying objects from her birth country to have around the house, getting special clothing for her to wear to International Day at school, regularly cooking regional food, and always talking about her birth country. We thought it would be nice to visit there once every year or two, to allow the country to feel familiar to her, to learn the language, and to make her feel that this was also her home. Alas, every time we suggested visiting, we were met with a resounding "Nooo!" We would have to wait until she was ready.

One day, around five years after we'd brought her home, she decided she'd like to go to "her country". We had done nothing different. She just felt ready, and we were relieved. She even discussed going to see her birth family.

As luck would have it, we were unable to travel that year. The following year, we were informed that her birth mother had died. *Shit.* We had missed the chance for her to meet the person who gave her life, the person she will probably always wonder about. We were devastated; we still are.

When we told her the news, bracing ourselves for the reaction, we learned a very important lesson: Children take in what they can at different stages in their lives, and you can never assume their understanding of any given situation.

Years ago, we'd bought a beautiful silk photo album in her birth country for the most special photos: those we managed to take of the centre, the nannies and the people who ran the centre, and her birth family. We would go through it with her and tell stories of the people and the places. We did this quite often in the first couple of years after bringing her home. Then normal life took over, and we rarely got the photo album out. I assumed that she remembered all of the stories and the people we had looked at and talked about.

On hearing the news of her birth mother's death, she asked to see a photo of her, so we looked through the album. She couldn't remember any of the people in it, but when we got to a photo of two tiny puppies, she remembered the story I had told her about them. I was shocked; then I laughed at myself. Adults so often project their own thoughts and feelings onto a child. They assume the same level of understanding or importance placed on certain things. I'd assumed that because I knew all of the stories and had told them to her when she was really quite little, that they would be of vital importance to her. Then I realised that her life, at this time, was about playing, eating, sleeping, having fun at school with her friends and feeling safe with her family. And *we* provided all of that.

No doubt, at a later stage in her life, this loss will come up and affect her in a different way, just as each thing has done so far, as she develops her understanding of the world and of her own situation.

I feel the sadness, the loss, the grief that she will never get to meet such an important person. But she doesn't feel the full force of it yet, and maybe she never will. But that's the thing, isn't it – who knows?

Never assume you know what your child is thinking and feeling. She is on her own journey, and we are just there to support her.

Birth Family Visits

It was a bit surreal to realise we had finally pulled off the birth family trip we had imagined for so long. Our girl had now met some of her birth family.

We had originally planned to bring our girl's grandmother and sibling to the country next to theirs, where it was easier for us to fly in and travel with small children. This two-person trip soon turned into a six-person trip, however, as her birth family were excited to have an excursion when they'd never been far from their own village before. We now had six passports ready, for Grandma, Aunty, Uncle, sibling and two small cousins.

We decided against taking her back to her birth country for this visit, and despite the work involved in organising the trip for the birth family, I stand by my decision. I was uneasy about returning to her birth country. Safety was an issue, and we didn't have an embassy there. Despite the fact that my husband and I had travelled there many times to see them since we adopted our girl, knowing we would have four little ones with us meant my appetite for adventure was much reduced.

It had taken about eight months to arrange the documentation remotely: passports, birth certificates, yellow fever vaccination certificates, flights, hotel bookings, ID cards. It was an administrative nightmare of epic proportions, comparable only to the original adoption process.

The plan was that we would fly in first and get settled. We decided not to tell our girl that her birth family was coming. I worried that something would go wrong that would prevent them from turning up, so I merely made out that we were having a family weekend away. I was planning on mentioning, very casually, that we should call Grandma and her brother to see if they wanted to join us for a few days, once we had boarded and were on our way.

The night before they arrived, I decided to check them all in online. I'd written very detailed explanatory instructions – imagine you'd never flown on a plane before. I told them to be at the airport four hours before (just to be safe), and to carry with them a small bag with food for the baby, a nappy, and some toys for the kids, as well as a list of other essentials. I explained that they would go to a desk and hand over their clothes bag to go on to the plane, and that they would then go through a machine at security. I told them that they were not allowed to take water with them, but they would get this for free on the plane, and that food was also free on the plane so they should eat it. I made sure to tell them that there is, in fact, somewhere to go to the toilet on the plane.

I was impressed that we'd managed to get this far together. As I checked them in online, however, I saw to my dismay that Grandma had been assigned a seat at the back of the plane, on her own. I burst out: "Oh no, Grandma is on her own at the back!" My daughter picked up on this instantly, and asked if her grandmother was coming.

I tried to keep my cool and act as if it was no big deal. I said something about having casually mentioned that we might be in a neighbouring country, if they fancied meeting up for a coffee. I never mentioned that I had worked hard for over eight months to prepare the family to meet us; I just said to my daughter that we would call when we got there and see if they fancied joining us!

We had booked a small, traditional hotel that only had about eight rooms, all of which opened up onto a courtyard. We thought this would work better, with all the kids interacting and us all hanging out rather than being confined to a small bedroom for the entire weekend.

They weren't arriving till late, so I put the kids to bed and my mum stayed and looked after them while my husband and I went to collect the family from the airport in the van. At this stage, I was still worried about whether they would even have been able to board the plane and survive the journey. When we saw them come through Arrivals, it was so emotional. They looked overwhelmed. They started doing a dance and came running over to us, placing a tribal hat on my husband as a sign of respect that he was the head of the family. They immediately passed me the baby, and we ushered them into the waiting van to take them back to the hotel.

While the language barrier can be hard, it is amazing in these situations how you can understand so much when you're only getting a word here and there. Smiles and hugs and "hallelujah" told us they were delighted and emotional to be with us.

On arrival, we asked them if they wanted to wake up our girl, and they were excited. They walked into the dark hotel room where she and her sister were sleeping, and started shouting "hallelujah" and dancing, using the drawers and walls as drums. My girl woke up, a bit startled, and I introduced her to her grandmother. She jumped out of bed and they all hugged. It was all a bit surreal. I had to walk out; they were so excited, but my emotions were so mixed. I felt sad, overwhelmed, worried about whether I'd done the right thing, as well as proud that I had pulled it off. We ordered them some food, the kids went back to bed, and we suggested we all get some sleep before the morning.

When we all woke, they were mesmerised by everything. They very quickly saw their/our girl as caretaker of the family, and expected her to look after her six-month-old cousin. She had to hold him whilst she ate her breakfast, carry him on her back in a sling, and take care of everything for the weekend. She loved this responsibility but, I must admit, it made me a bit uncomfortable. The attitude towards a nine-year-old child was so starkly different between our two cultures.

Funnily enough, the bond that I thought would be instant between our girl and her twin wasn't as natural as I had expected. It was as if she had met him now, and had ticked a box. Our biological son was far more interested in him, and the two of them quickly grew close. Despite my son being four years younger than the twin, they were the same size. They became like long-lost cousins, and it was amazing to see how they could spend hours interacting without being able to communicate.

My girl amused me and slightly embarrassed me that weekend. Of all of my children, she behaved the most "Western", constantly asking for hand sanitiser. She was on a little holiday with these biological family members who shared little with her apart from blood. I found this strange; I had expected their biology to create an instant connection and understanding. Part of me was quietly pleased that she *did* feel like she belonged to us, though; that our love and parenting over the years had meant so much in these moments. I was proud of all of them, and how they handled the situation.

The weekend was a huge success and a real "bucket list" thing for me. I feel like it gave her some closure. She appeared very unfazed by the whole thing, but I think it answered a lot of questions for her. It allowed her to see that these people we had spoken about for so long were real.

She hit a bit of an emotional low a few weeks after returning. She didn't really speak about it much, but I could see it was on her mind. I only hope that in years to come, she can verbalise how she felt about it all a bit more, and give me a little glimmer of hope that it was the right thing to do.

Returning to Your Child's Birth Country

My husband and I aren't big planners. We never really plan anything, and leave everything to the last minute. So when it came to dealing with our son's questions and adoption issues, we, of course, had no plan. All we'd decided to do was to answer any questions as openly, gently and honestly as we could whenever things came up – hopefully tailoring it so that it was appropriate to his developmental stage. We had always assumed we would take family trips to his birth country as often as we could, to allow our son to get to know his country. We had also assumed that, at some stage, he would want to meet his birth family, and we were completely fine with that.

I'd met his birth family during the adoption process, as this was required by our visa process. Because of this, I had photos and stories to tell our son. Each case is different, though, and many people have no story to tell their children when it comes to their birth family. I felt lucky that I was able to honestly and clearly answer many of the questions our son asked – even though this brings with it complications.

The questions and feelings that arise each year from our son fascinate me. It so clearly demonstrates his level of understanding as it develops, and allows me to get a little bit of insight into what is going on inside his head.

For years, our son was petrified of visiting his country. He was unable to verbalise exactly what he was scared of, so we left it alone and hoped he would one day be ready.

That day came when he was about eight years old, when he announced proudly: "I would like to go and see my country!" Not wanting to make too much of this, we all agreed that it would be great to visit soon, and talked about how lovely it would be to eat the food and see the beautiful countryside. We deliberately didn't mention his birth family, as we didn't want to make him nervous about the trip. We figured that when we were there and had settled in, we would very casually ask him if he would like to visit them.

A couple of days after his announcement, while I was brushing his teeth, he said, "My birth family will be so happy to see me – they will say, 'You got so big!'" He hadn't mentioned anything about his birth family before, and I didn't know whether he'd thought about seeing them; but here he was, all relaxed and happy about it – certain they would be excited to see him.

We had a few quick conversations about the visit, but one conversation in particular left me in awe. Our son often has a hard time constructing sentences and finding the right words to describe things. But on that particular evening, he spoke so eloquently and with such maturity. He asked to look at his "special album" – an album that has photos of the hospital where he was born, of rivers and villages on the way out to his birthplace, the chief's house, the whole village, the huts and various members of his birth family, including extended family. It is very special to him, and I feel very lucky that he has something concrete to look at.

After going through the photos, I asked how he was feeling about the upcoming trip. "Nervous and excited," was his answer. He then went on to talk for two hours. It was incredible. He discussed feeling lonely inside because he felt so disconnected from his birth family. He said he was nervous because he didn't know how they felt about him. We discussed how we thought they might react when they saw him. I explained that our cultures were very different and that they had lived a very different life, so they may behave a little differently to what we would.

Both of us cried while discussing these deeply emotional topics. I have never felt closer to him than during that conversation. He asked to sleep with me that night, so he would feel safe and loved. In the morning, he hugged me tightly and told me that he loved me and his daddy and brother and sisters so much, and that he was happy he was in this family and that he never wanted us to die. His reaction was helping me to feel that we were all very ready to make the trip to his birth country.

The two days leading up to the trip were filled with him saying he was so nervous, he felt he couldn't go. He said he wished he had gone earlier. I explained that he hadn't been ready earlier, and that if he didn't go now, it would just build up and get even more nerve-wracking! He agreed, as he was desperate to go – just extremely nervous.

So we went. Our dear friends from the centre were kind enough to take us to his birth family's village and translate for us. We went on the first day, which I was so glad about – my husband and son were both so nervous that we wouldn't have been able to enjoy anything until we had done this.

The long drive out from the capital city went quite quickly as we discussed the sights, sounds and smells. When we arrived, our boy clung to me like a monkey. He wrapped himself around me and tried to hide his face. My husband immediately greeted his birth father and sat beside him. To say that it was awkward is an understatement. Everyone was embarrassed and shy, and yet wanted so badly to see and communicate with each other.

Our little boy met his birth family. There were no words spoken between them, just long looks and a little bit of touch. We told them all about their/our son's life, and what he enjoyed doing. We asked questions about their lives. Our boy grew more comfortable with every passing minute. Still shy, but wanting to connect with these people, he looked at them and smiled and looked down, over and over again. We were with them for hours, most of which was spent standing still, just looking and smiling.

When it was time to leave, we said our goodbyes and drove away. I cuddled our boy and asked how he was feeling. "I wish I could have stayed longer," was his answer. My husband and I were both so relieved it had gone well, and that he'd felt welcome and comfortable there.

We have always wanted him to feel comfortable in his birth country, and proud of his story – where he came from and why he came to be with us. He has since voiced his desire to learn his language, so that he'll be able to speak to his brothers. We have always thought this would be a good idea; it's just hard to find a teacher where we live. But we will find a way for him to learn.

He spoke of the way they live and how he could live there perfectly well. He, who now has a privileged upbringing, would love nothing more than to sleep on the floor and play in the dirt. It is so deeply a part of who he is, and we do not aim to change him in any way (except maybe encourage table manners!). We love and respect that he is genetically different from us, and that he comes from another world. We understand that he will feel torn and confused at various times in his life, but I hope he will also feel lucky – lucky that he has the chance to choose his path in life. Whether he decides to visit his country often, live there, work there, or never go there again, we will support him. All I want is for him to feel proud of who he is – *all* of who he is. We do.

I think this trip has answered a whole heap of his questions, but it will also bring up a whole lot more. As this happened only recently, I feel he is still processing everything that he saw and felt. I know that things will come up soon, and I'll be happy to deal with them as our son makes sense of his life, his roots and the meaning of the word "family".

◆ ◆ ◆

Here are some suggestions for birth country visits:

◈ I strongly encourage parents to wait until their child feels completely ready to visit their birth country and/or birth parents. If your child is very small, then visiting the country would be fine for them. But with children older than three, their awareness is great, but their understanding is lacking and their ability to vocalise how they are feeling is limited, so the trip may cause more harm than good.

◈ Discuss as much as you can with your child before travelling. Encourage open conversations, leaving all judgment behind. Allow your child to express all of their feelings, whether they make sense to you or not, and regardless of whether they may hurt you.

◈ Ensure the birth family has been asked if they are OK with seeing your child. Do not promise your child that they will meet them until it has been confirmed and arranged, and even then, be a little cautious about overpromising.

◈ Discuss a range of possible reactions from birth parents. Your child may be expecting a tearful, giant hug reunion, which may not be the case.

◈ Try your best to be open to any reaction from your child when they visit their birth country and/or birth parents. This could range from tears, wanting to stay with them, not wanting to see them, extreme confusion and strange behaviour, anger, hurt. The list is endless. This is a *huge* thing for our children. It is striking deep into the very core of their being. Allow them time to process it all, and be open at any time for discussion.

◈ Take lots of photos. Your child may have no interest in looking at them in the short term, but will likely appreciate them at a later stage. Taking them will save any trouble later.

◈ Remember, children do not belong to us – they are with us to love, protect and guide, not cling to. Accept their feelings, and love them regardless.

Different Behavioural Challenges

———◇———

"There is one more piece of advice I have for you: don't get impatient. Even if things are so tangled up you can't do anything, don't get desperate or blow a fuse or start yanking on one particular thread before it's ready to come undone. You have to realize it's going to be a long process and that you'll work on things slowly, one at a time."

Haruki Murakami

———◇———

Section Contents

The Trials and Tribulations of Discipline

If your adopted child is your first child, you are likely to have plenty of false starts with discipline.

If your adopted child isn't your first child, you are likely to have plenty of false starts with discipline.

Let's address the first category: take the parenting methods you were subject to as a child, have observed in other families, or thought you would follow, and throw them out the window. Any sense that you would have a "one-size-fits-all" approach to discipline is also likely to be flawed. Further, any approach that works well with your child today, is likely to have a fairly short use-by date.

Our biggest challenge with our introduction to parenting was that our kids were not attached at all to us, let alone to things. If I expressed upset or disappointment, they would look right through me, smile and ask me to play with them or make them a snack, having no idea that they were in my bad books. When we moved on to the removal of a privilege – not seeing a friend, or not getting an ice-cream that had been promised – again we would be met with the child equivalent of a shrug.

We then tried to take things away temporarily and have the kids earn them back. Said toy or special dress would sit on my shelf indefinitely. In the early days, I ended up collecting a bin bag full of dresses, shoes and clothes. The kids showed no interest in getting them back. Again, a figurative shrug.

When one of the kids was suspended from preschool because he couldn't listen to the teacher, the director of the school asked us to attend a positive parenting course. The main thing I remember from that course is that the teacher mispronounced a word she chose to use incessantly, which was distracting as we were both so focused on not giggling. We attempted to put the things we'd learned into practice, and tried to praise the children when they did the right thing. They seemed to enjoy the positive attention, but it didn't move the dial at all in terms of creating the right behavioural patterns. We tried reward charts. We tried star charts. We tried earning TV time and later, as technology advanced, earning iPad time. I've been crouched down, holding my child's hand and telling her I love her and calmly asking her not to pee on the floor when she's angry, and that there would be no TV that day if she did. She would just as calmly look me in the eye and start peeing.

Positive parenting, or other parenting methods that may work for securely attached children, will rarely work with children who have attachment issues. Don't let childcare experts try to convince you otherwise. Quite possibly they might work, and certainly there are components that will work, but you need to follow your gut with your child.

With one child who was struggling with violence and aggression, we tried a raft of methods with little success. The one that had some impact was bribing her to behave. If she had a day without a bad outburst, she'd get a tick, and when she had a certain number of ticks she'd get to do something awesome. We went to a water park and swimming with dolphins, which she loved and got some sense of achievement and success from; but I know that when she was having a bad day, the thought of missing a tick mattered little.

With another child, we tried to use the naughty step, or "thinking step". This was the discipline method *du jour* when this child was young, but it was absolutely ineffective. He never screamed or tried to get off. He would walk over to it and sit down calmly, not at all bothered. Because I was raising numerous kids who were fairly intense, I would often move on to the next issue and forget he was there for a while. I have distinct memories of him falling asleep happily on the naughty step. I don't like the step method. Certainly, if you do use it, you should rename it as it's not great to label a child as naughty, especially adopted kids. It's a similar story with sending them to their room. We do that now with fairly attached kids, but in the early days, it smacks of rejection and doesn't encourage the unconditional love and acceptance you are trying to show your child.

The frustration at not being able to find anything, literally *anything*, that would encourage the right behaviours was grating. We'd often come to each other with a fantastic idea, convinced that *this* was what would make a difference. We'd implement it and watch it start out OK, and swiftly crash and burn.

My frustration led to some questionable behaviour on my part. The strangest, most emotionally volatile thing I recall doing was taking a pair of scissors to my preschooler's princess high heels and cutting off the cute fluffy bit on the front. She watched me, confused. Even my adoptive mother friends, who always listen without judgement, raised their eyebrows at this one. Not my finest parenting moment.

For years we searched and really, we never found anything. It was not until the children were securely attached that we could speak to them about expectations and disappointment, that we had much influence at all. And along the way, we adjusted, learned to pick our battles and to lower our expectations around behaviour. We also learned a lot about forgiveness and truly unconditional love. We're still learning.

For adoptive parents who have other children, you may have read this and thought that some of these discipline strategies will indeed work for you, as they have with your other children. The big difference is that your adopted children don't have the rock solid bond that your biological children had. Well-attached and adjusted kids simply need to hear parental disappointment or disapproval, or joy and approval, to respond. It takes years to build this relationship with your adoptive child, so be prepared to adjust your methods.

◆   ◆   ◆

Here are some ideas to try when it comes to disciplining your child:

◊   Focus first and foremost on attachment. Without that, no discipline method you attempt will have any meaningful impact, and you will simply churn from one method to the next.

◊   Be clear about your expectations and remind your child of them often. Particularly before you're about to go out, or to school, or watch a movie, take the time to talk about how they should behave when they're in that situation.

◊   Praise your child more than you think is reasonable when they do behave well. When we feel our parenting is getting too negative, we try to remember to say three positive things for each negative thing.

◊   If you want to try reward systems (and we have, with varied results – they never last long), make the rewards very tangible and very short term. Impulse control and delayed gratification are likely to be things your child struggles with, so getting a reward a week into the future can be hard for them to get excited about.

◊   When you are disciplining your child, remember to talk about their behaviour, not about them as a person. Use phrases like: "I always love you, but I don't like it when you behave angrily towards me and push me."

What's Yours Is Mine: Stealing

It was his sister's birthday and I hadn't had time to take him shopping to choose a present for her. I had plenty for her, though, and simply requested he make a card. He did, and it was sweet, but my maternal pride skyrocketed when she realised there was $20 in the card. He explained, "I didn't get you a present, so I wanted to give you some of my money instead." I questioned where he'd got it from, but his explanation that he found it in his old wallet was plausible. We all waxed lyrical about how kind and generous this act was.

Later that day, as we prepared to go out, I was switching things from my big work bag into my weekend bag, transferring the cash I'd withdrawn the night before. But there didn't seem to be enough there. I went onto the Internet to double-check how much I'd withdrawn, mentally retraced my steps since stopping at the ATM, and concluded something was amiss.

After a little discussion, I'd narrowed it down to him. The other kids are far from perfect, but they are terrible liars, while he is a master of deception when he needs to be. He pleaded and cried that it wasn't him, that he really had just found it. My husband and I knew it was him, though – his responses to our questioning were taking a form we were familiar with. He'd say "no" and then cave a little to a different question, his adamant "no" meaning something far more pliable to him. Eventually, perhaps an hour later, we determined that he'd taken several hundred dollars from my purse, and snuck to the newsagent to buy football trading cards with the money. He'd asked me if he could run around the block. (No wonder the local newsagent is always so friendly to him.)

When something like this happens, I try not to lose my cool, and given this was another child's birthday, we really had to stay cool. The frustration, anger and disappointment at this behaviour does eat at you, though. It makes you question all you do with your kids, to imagine a sad future visiting your child in the local jail. And it's hard not to judge the child harshly – by my moral code, you do not steal money from your mother's purse, buy junk with it, lie about it, and then bask in the adoration you receive when you give a tiny bit of your loot to your sister.

When we looked in his room, there were ripped-open packets from the trading cards everywhere, stuffed into the crevices of drawers and boxes. He had to stack them all up and give them to me. I put them away in my upstairs bedroom, and told him I didn't trust him to use my iPad, or to come upstairs to my bedroom.

A week or two later, I was working from home and therefore able to pick up the kids. I look forward to this, though I don't get to do it often. It's a very concrete way to feel connected with the kids during the week, when they are at school and doing their activities, and I'm usually commuting into the city, most weeks travelling interstate or having a dinner or two out, and returning tired. As I walked through the playground to get my younger child, I saw him outside a classroom on the receiving end of a talking-to from a teacher. This got my senses heightened, and as we walked down to his classroom, I saw him come out and immediately have three or four boys surround him. They were arguing with him, and clearly it was about those stupid trading cards. One of the boys said he'd taken one of his. I raised an eyebrow and held my hand out. He handed me a stack of cards.

"Where did you get these?" I asked him.

"Your room," he admitted.

I was glad we were at school and I couldn't yell. I took them off him and gave the other boy the card he was claiming, and tried to give the boys all of the cards. They backed away from the crazy mother lady and went on their way.

My boy got a piece of my mind that afternoon.

When they've gotten into big trouble not once, but twice, most kids know they are on thin ice and work hard to do the right thing. Not this kid.

That weekend, I made a cake, as I often do. I chose this particular cake simply for its ability to underpin cream cheese icing. The cake was rustic and good, full of cinnamon and apple, and served still slightly warm. We each ate a little and put the rest in the fridge, knowing we'd have the same on Sunday afternoon.

On Sunday, we were having a relaxed day. I didn't want to go far, as I was travelling a lot the next week, and we had family visiting. As I opened the fridge, the cake caught my eye. For a moment, I thought the icing had melted, as we hadn't let it cool fully before we'd iced it. Then I noticed a small hand-sized chunk ripped off the top, and I knew what had happened. I asked him straight away, and he confessed fairly quickly. After this run of poor behaviour, my anger was far reduced. I simply told him to go outside out of my sight for a little while, and that I didn't like stealing and greed.

When he came back in, I explained to him that he was going to make a cake for the family that day, clean up the mess, and not eat any himself. With a little supervision from me, we made a Greek yoghurt cheesecake with a shortbread crust. It was good. I hugged him as we calmly made it, and said we all make mistakes and your family still loves you, even when you mess up. And that I still wasn't giving him any of it until he had shown better behaviour, maybe by the following afternoon.

It's our pattern that if he behaves badly, my blood boils, but he quickly settles back to his now more even-tempered self. It would be so easy to look at him and forgive his indiscretions, but I know better. For bigger screw-ups, we execute simple, consequence-based strategies. With adopted kids, finding consequences that have impact can be hard, as they are especially good at showing little response to consequences. But you figure them out eventually. For him, it's time with no iPad or TV, much tighter supervision and less trust, and direct consequences, like making the cake.

For the money he'd stolen, I deducted the balance from the "Mummy bank" – an iPhone note that adds up the kids' weekly pocket money, deducts amounts used to buy something, and deals with debt repayment. Then, he had to make the choices about when and how to repay the money. It took several months, but we've done this before a couple of times. When we're out at a café and the other kids are having a milkshake, for example, I'll remind him of his debt and give him a choice. He'll often (but not always) choose debt repayment. The iPhone note is a simple and effective strategy that works for us.

I hate stealing and I hate lying, but I love my child. It's hard. Changing these behaviours takes years and years. Stay strong, and stay patient.

Lies, Omissions and Twisted Tales

It was New Year's Eve, and we were on holidays at the beach: the days a blur of sun, ocean, reading, playing with new Christmas toys, and resting. The family was peaceful, the rented house had plenty of space, and the days were long and deliciously warm.

One of the kids loved singing, so Santa had gifted her a microphone with an SD card loaded full of karaoke songs. All you needed was a TV to plug it in to (have karaoke, will travel!). Hence our plan for New Year's Eve was to have dinner, dessert and fizzy drink, and then sing karaoke until midnight, or when we crashed. The kids were excited, and I was relieved we'd decided against going out in search of fireworks and getting caught up in the inevitable crowds.

I prepared dinner as the rest of the family read, watched movies and chatted happily. We set the table on the worn-out but wonderful wooden sundeck: cutlery, party hats, plates, cups, fizzy drink. Er, who drank half of the fizzy drink, guys?

The littlest one, only four and refreshingly straightforward, says it wasn't her, and we believe her. The older one, who has trouble with the truth, assures us it wasn't her and we believe her, too – she doesn't have a sweet tooth. So the middle one it must be. But she denies and denies to the point of extreme frustration for us, particularly as it is on a night when we are in a party mood and have no interest at all in getting upset with anyone.

We stated all the usual, well-worn caveats, starting out gently and then getting grumpier.

You'll get in more trouble for lying than for what you actually did, we're not actually that upset about the fizzy drink, but we do need you to tell the truth.

Telling the truth is an important part of our family.

Sometimes it can be hard to get out of things, can't it? I can help you get back on track.

If you won't tell the truth, there will be consequences for you.

Right then, that's it. There will be no fizzy drink for you.

Still, nada. She had no soft drink that night while the other kids indulged. She knew that a confession would be quickly forgiven, and still chose to stay quiet. We know our kids well, and when one of them is lying, it's fairly evident to us. This is but one example of a scenario that plays out for us very regularly.

◆　◆　◆

I have a child who goes through spurts of serial, inconsequential, pointless and fanciful lying.

She doesn't lie about practical matters, like who drank the soft drink. Hers are interpersonal lies, lies by omission, and twisted information. She will answer a different question to the one I ask, twist the truth, leave significant things out, or slowly reveal information. For a person who prides herself on being direct and transparent, this behaviour is excruciating for me. She gets a short-term boost but a long-term problem; she knows that, but seems hard-wired to continue with this behaviour.

This child of ours has been with us a long time. Her logical brain knows lying is wrong, and for a while now, we have been generously and deliberately rewarding truth-telling even when it's difficult.

She also knows in her logical brain that we are well-connected to her school community and we will find out soon enough if she's been lying, and call her out immediately. And she also knows that the other girls at school will brand her a liar, and this will make it even more difficult than it already is for her to make and keep friends.

And yet every few months, we're back to this conversation, having learned of some new, highly inventive yarn she's spun.

I struggle to understand this behaviour; both my husband and I are honest to a fault. Truth is valued above all other attributes in our family. She'll now generally tell me and her dad the truth, as she knows we will quickly uncover falsehoods, omissions and half-truths. But outside of the family, in the heat of the moment and wanting to sound interesting to a new friend or to avoid a more difficult conversation, she'll say anything she feels like.

It's about attention, about fitting in, and then it becomes about not being able to extract herself or unwind her story once she's started.

We only ever find out about these lies when we're speaking to other people. Does your child have cancer? Do you have cancer? Are you leaving her home alone so you can go away for the weekend? We were praying in class today for her twin brother and his gender reassignment surgery (no twin, no gender reassignment). I wish I was making this up.

◆ ◆ ◆

My favourite is when my son does something right in front of me and when I question him, he flatly and fully denies ever doing it. At first, I would argue back: "But I was watching you do it!" This only led to more denial and maternal frustration! Then I started answering his initial denial with, "You're right. I must be mistaken." This confuses him, and he ends up admitting what he did. I take a similar approach when he's doing something to annoy me, like dragging his trainers on the floor of the mall so they make a horrid squeaking sound. If I ask him to stop, he will happily keep it up for as long as possible. If I tell him, "I love it when you make that sound. Can you do it more? Can you do it louder?" he whines "*M-U-U-U-M-M-M!*" and instantly stops. Reverse psychology at its best!

◆ ◆ ◆

The truth is a tricky thing to teach children who nod their heads as you bestow life lessons on them and then, once your back is turned for a second, are off telling porky pies again. And they're often not big or important lies but silly, inconsequential ones, that make you think the payoff cannot be worth it. The kids know they are very likely to be caught out, that we won't brush it under the carpet, and that there will be consequences. And yet still...

This behaviour is frustrating for parents, but of course it also has ramifications that will hurt your child in time. Friendships are harder to sustain, particularly as they get older, when your child chooses to be liberal with the truth. Friends start to say that they can't trust them as they never tell the truth. But to some kids, it's second nature.

It's high-intensity parenting to try to stem this behaviour. Here are some tips that have helped us:

◊ We help the kids try to understand why they might feel lying is easier than telling the truth. Your child lies for a reason: to please someone else, or seek attention or make themselves seem exciting, or to avoid disappointing someone. These are all the behaviours of children with low self-esteem. You, of course, need to work on attachment and building self-esteem. Also explain to them that it's more important to be themselves and say what they really think than to tell someone what they want to hear, and that they will still be loved and valued.

◊ All this explaining and rationalising can take a while – years, many years – to translate into change. The high-intensity part comes from the need to act like a detective, asking questions and checking that the answer is correct. Did you wash your hands? Show me. Did you brush your teeth? Let me smell. Did you unpack your lunchbox? Show me. Honestly, after a decade of parenting my kids, and them knowing I am relentless about the truth, I *still* cannot trust their answers.

◊ Create a few phrases that you repeat to the kids often – some "family slogans", for want of a better description. We regularly say to our kids that in our family, we tell the truth, that it is really important to us. We tell the truth even when it's hard or we're a bit scared of what the other person will say.

◈ Kids often need help when they've started to lie and are digging themselves a hole to stubbornly sit in with no ability to dig themselves out. They put up their emotional shutters and will bear *any* consequence rather than try to repair the issue. Over the years, we've learned that while we might feel angry and shouty, the best approach is to be gentle. We'll hold out the olive branch with a statement like, "Sometimes it's hard to get yourself out of a difficult situation, would you like my help?"

◈ Don't ask Yes/No questions. Adaptation often trains children not to admit to anything, even in the face of overwhelming evidence. Try asking a question that assumes the answer you are looking for. For example, instead of "Did you eat some biscuits?", you ask "How did you like the biscuits?" You're far more likely to get a straight answer.

◈ Children will often tell tall tales to get out of perceived trouble. Adopted children can develop finely honed storytelling skills. As previously stated, children with a history of trauma cannot access their rational brain when they're stressed, so you are wasting your time trying to demonstrate the illogicality of their answers. Better to wait until they, and you, are calm.

◈ If the truth only comes after a dance, we'll say thank you for being honest. We'll also speak about the importance of being honest right away, and how that builds trust. Reiterating the need for honesty is vital in emotionally-charged moments, but also in day-to-day moments. I'll make a point of telling the kids stories about when I was really honest at work and how it was hard, but it was right.

◈ Reward truth-telling, no matter how hard. Even if it's a confession of poor behaviour, make it absolutely clear that they're getting into *less* trouble because they told the truth. Try to do this consistently over the years, as truth-telling can wax and wane and needs constant reinforcement. I try to thank the kids for telling me the truth each and every time they do this.

◇ Be unshockable. This is, in fact, a strategy I have adopted across all areas of my life in recent years – as the leader of a team of people at work, and as the mother of children. It is a vital skill to master for any variety of teenager you parent. I rate it highly, and always offer this as my first piece of teenage-parenting lore. The reason you have to be unshockable is so that the kids will always want to tell you things, no matter how scary, awful, silly or embarrassing. They know they will not get an overreaction and they will not get judgement. We will discuss things and I'll ask them to tell me what they think they should do before offering any ideas of my own. I have had many very shocking moments in my parenting journey. I have kept a poker face while my stomach twisted in knots and internally I howled with anger, upset or disappointment.

◇ Demystify mistake-making and failure. Popular culture is firmly focused on #slaying and #goals. You have to look a little harder to find people speaking openly and honestly about failure. I believe this is dangerous for general mental health in society, and I'm heartened by a newer trend for high profile people to speak about struggles they've had. Within your family, talk about mistakes you've made, the lessons you've learned and the fact that life went on after that mistake. One thing that can start you off is a dinner table prompt I read about on a blog called Rose, Bud and Thorn.[19] Each of you around the table talks about your favourite part of the day (the Rose), your least favourite part (the Thorn), and what you're looking forward to tomorrow (the Bud). We don't do it every night, but we do it often. I want the kids to see that each of us has difficult times.

◇ One of my kids lies because she is a people-pleaser, and is afraid to have an opinion or to go against the will of another. To help her with this, I have started to make sure I model healthy disagreement for her. I'll talk about disagreements at work, with a friend, or with my husband (always a lot of rich content in that relationship!). I encourage her not to be afraid of being her own person.

---

19 https://www.designmom.com/making-mealtimes-meaningful-take-the-challenge/

◊ As they get older, you need to give them slightly more sophisticated tools, by teaching them to differentiate between harmless lies to save someone's feelings and lies that aren't harmless. They need to learn that the truth can be brutal if dispensed too freely.

◊ If you're having serious issues eradicating lying behaviour, blitz it for a period. Set short-term goals and track those goals daily, then reward them with whatever motivates your child. It could be school lunch money, TV time, a visit to the skate park, a chocolate bar. This will encourage them to start associating the truth with feeling good.

◊ The book *When Love Is Not Enough*[20] suggests a novel game to get an older child to stop lying, and I tried it once. My child had regressed to lying every time he opened his mouth. As he was much older and I was parenting solo that week, I took unusual action. I told the other kids that every time their brother lied, they got a point. Whoever got the most points got a chocolate at the end of the day. He was horrified by this approach, and I assured him if he didn't lie all day then *he'd* get a chocolate. After about five days, he had gotten over that habit again.

◊ Build their self-esteem and teach them that true friends are those with whom you can be yourself and honest, so that they see themselves as inherently worthy of interest and do not need to resort to wildly fabricated stories. (I am guilty of embellishment for the sake of a good story, but it's always rooted in some truth: I've never had a brother going through gender reassignment, for example.)

---

20 *When Love Is Not Enough: A Guide to Parenting With RAD-Reactive Attachment Disorder*, Nancy Thomas. The approaches in this book can be controversial. Some of us have tried some of the methods in it and some have worked. Like all things adoption, we take the parts that work for us.

Selfishness and Revenge: Served Ice, Ice Cold

After a litany of misbehaviour that day, I sent my daughter to bed early. That was the last straw for her. She went, but took ages to wash and get ready.

The next morning, the sun streamed in early; we regrouped and hoped for a better day.

My husband brought up coffee while the kids slept in. I turned on the iPad, looking forward to reading some blogs or news until the littlest woke. As I reached for my coffee, the bedside table didn't look right. My engagement ring was missing.

My heart sank. I never, ever put it anywhere but on my finger, or on that table. I sprung up, my peaceful Sunday morning disturbed until I set this right. I looked in all the places I could make a case for; then I stopped and burst into tears. I do not attach easily to material things, but this ring is the single exception. I adore it. My husband started to look in places that didn't make sense. We rationalised that it had to be in the house somewhere; I clearly remembered putting it on the table the night before. But it wasn't showing up anywhere.

My tears rolled and rolled. I couldn't understand how it could have disappeared – unless one of the kids had moved it?

They were starting to wake and come upstairs, and were immediately upset to see me red-eyed. Each of them was steadfast that they had no idea where the ring was. I was getting suspicious and also mad, and got them searching high and low through the house. If I saw one of them start playing with a toy or sitting down, I'd bark at them that we *all* had to keep looking until the ring was found.

The search continued for a really long time, maybe an hour. I was feeling more and more distressed – maybe I hadn't put it on the bedside table? Maybe I'd lost it, or it was stolen while we were out and about?

My girl, who had been in my bad books the day before, kept going out to the laundry. I started to watch her more closely. After perhaps the third time she'd been in the laundry, she suggested I look there. Sure enough, there it was on the floor.

I cried, this time with relief, thanked the kids for helping me look, and tried to calm myself down.

I knew without a doubt that my girl had hidden my ring to scare me, to get some payback for giving her an early bedtime the night before. I asked nicely for her to admit it, but no luck. I asked a little more forcefully; nope, still innocent. Even by the time I was yelling, she assured me it wasn't her. I knew it was best to leave her and then come back to it later.

I did so, on several occasions, and got the same answer every time. It's years later now, and she has still not confessed that she did this.

Some of our kids dish out payback that would make Tony Soprano proud. After a fight with a sibling, one of the kids wiped their butt with the other's toothbrush. I wish I was joking; it still makes me feel queasy. In the child's eyes, this was a reasonable response to a perceived slight. (Thankfully, the toothbrush owner smelt something was up before actually using it.)

◆ ◆ ◆

Here are a few ways to encourage forgiveness and eliminate the scorekeeping kids can become obsessed with:

◈ Model forgiveness yourself. Use phrases like, "What you did hurt my feelings, but I love you and forgive you." Or even, "I'm going to need some time to forgive you, but I love you."

◈ Speak to your child when you feel angry with someone else and want revenge. Show them the feelings are very real, and how to moderate them.

◈ Coach your kids to speak with each other and discuss their issues, rather than punch each other when you're not looking. Sit with them and work through it, talk-show-host style.

◈ Speak to your child about how others use words, not payback, for righting wrongs. Your child's school principal will not look kindly upon and likely find it hard to understand their medieval sense of justice. At the same time, though, we teach our kids to defend and stick up for themselves if they are being picked on. There's a fine line between using your words and being a pushover.

◈ When they do use their words to resolve a wrongdoing, praise them effusively for it.

◈ If the payback is really disproportionate, use consequence-based parenting and have the child do something as a consequence of their actions, possibly something for the other child.

Mum, I'm Hungry, Hungry, Hungry

Amongst our adopted kids, it's fascinating to observe that although they all started from a similar place in life, they each have a vastly different relationship with food.

For one of the kids, food equals routine and home. When she first came to us, the provision of regular hot meals three times a day meant security for her, a predictable routine, a promise that she could rely on us. As she's gotten older, food is quite sentimental to her – she'll often ask for or cook food from her birth country. The other kids love it. One of her most loved gifts from us was a cookbook of recipes from West Africa. When she eats the food of her earliest years, she'll often tell us a few stories we didn't know before, as the tastes and smells trigger memories for her.

Now that she's been with us for so long, there is a whole history developing around food for our family. It includes the prawns she ate at every opportunity for a few years, to the extent that we used to joke about whether she alone was going to cause the overfishing (or is it overprawning?) of the species. It includes the Malaysian laksa we all love: she always laughs about the day her dad's chopsticks accidentally flicked some of the soup into her face. It's Nigella's chocolate cloud cake that she requests me to make now and then. It's her dad's apple crumble with lashings of custard on rainy winter Sundays. It's the supermarket-bought Victoria sponge they are all obsessed with for family day (which we'll talk more about later – it's the day the kids were adopted or came home. We have a simple cake to mark the occasion each year). This one goes against my belief special cakes should be mum-made, but it's become the family day go-to cake.

Given her sentimentality around food memories, another of her most treasured gifts is a blank family recipe book. We filled some of it in for her, starting with my Christmas rum balls and my husband's much-loved shortbread. We added my mother's Singapore noodles and her mother's rice custard. The recipe book represents a new treasury of food memories being made that will one day take her right back to her childhood.

◆ ◆ ◆

Another of the girls is very different: to her, food is fuel. While she loves anything fried (and what on this earth doesn't taste better fried?) and has an endless appetite for cinnamon donuts, she could take or leave food many days. She'll eat so little over the course of a few days that I'll start getting concerned, and then eat loads a few days following. She seems to get what she needs when you average things out, so I've stopped worrying about her.

◆ ◆ ◆

Another child had a different story altogether: classic adopted child food issues.

When we first met him, he was always hungry. First thing each morning, he'd rifle through our bag to find the food we'd bought to the centre that day, demolish it and then ask for more.

We arranged a birthday/farewell party for him before we took him home, and it was fantastic: fifty kids eating, drinking and dancing their little hearts out. All except my boy – he simply ate and ate and ate. Every time I looked, he had a chicken drumstick in each hand. We weren't allowed to take him with us until the next day. When we returned to pick him up, the nurse told us how worried she'd been, as he'd been really ill all night from overindulging.

When we took him home, he was starving. He ate everything on his plate and always asked for more.

One evening, after the kids had brushed their teeth, he started chewing again as I read them a story. I noticed it, but didn't really register it. The next night, one of the other kids noticed, too, and we figured he'd stored food from dinner in his cheek, kept it there a few hours, managed to keep it in there through tooth brushing, and then started to enjoy his dinner again at storytime. It took months to break this habit – I'd check his little cheeks each night, but sometimes, if I was distracted with something else, he'd manage to get past me.

Years after being home and having ample amounts of food, he was still starving – or so he thought. Every breakfast, lunch and dinner he would request more, more, more! He would eat double or triple what grown adults did. We spoke to him about there always being enough food. We tried to get him tuned in with his body, to learn the feeling of full. We worked with him to slow down and chew properly – most of the time, he hardly chewed, he was in such a hurry to transport food from mouth to tummy. We spoke with him about the need to chew and showed him how to do it, and for how long. The chewing lesson ended up being quite comical. I exaggerated chewing for him, really moving my mouth and jaw around in slow motion. For a couple of years after this, whenever I told him to chew his food, he would mimic this. It sounds funny, but it was another hard habit to break.

One Sunday brunch, we'd grilled sausages, which all of the kids loved. The others ate two or three each, while my hungry boy had six and continued asking for more. I knew he wouldn't be able to eat so many; I argued with him, he started sulking, and I got fed up with the daily display of greed.

"How many more do you want?" I asked him.

"Five," he said.

"Fine, but if I give you five sausages, you'll sit here until they're eaten, OK?"

He was at that table for perhaps another hour, trying to prove me wrong, and succeeding at making himself feel sick. It was not a parenting moment I am proud of, but I was so fed up of not getting through. And no, this didn't do much for the cause, apart from create a funny story the kids bring up now and then.

Even several more years after coming home, he was *still* hungry. He'd sometimes wake up at night and rummage through the cupboards or fridge for something. We tried to counteract this by putting a Tupperware box of crackers and fruit next to his bed, hoping it would provide comfort that there was food right there if he needed it and stop him waking up. It simply encouraged him to wake up each night, to demolish the contents of the box.

Now, nearly ten years later, time has done its job and calmed him down. There wasn't a lot we did that created the change, in my view. It took years for him to trust that food supply would be steady. Even today, he can have some weird food issues, but no more so now than any of us.

◆ ◆ ◆

When another child came home, she'd tasted little apart from rice and cassava leaves, even though she was nearly three. She wanted everything she ate to be super spicy.

We were patient with her, and within weeks she was eating what we gave her for dinner. I soon learned that she would eat my cooking if I put Tabasco sauce on it. Dinner was at a table, with us attempting to teach some manners. However, every meal served in those early days landed up on a wall, over the newborn asleep in the corner, or on the floor.

Snack and lunch times were a different story. While our other child would snack on a bowl of grapes or berries, a piece of cheese or some yoghurt, this child would sit and hold her bowl (often for over an hour) and wouldn't touch, let alone taste, anything in it. I decided to let them eat snacks in the playroom, so that I wasn't watching them so closely and making a big deal out of it. It took months, but she slowly began to take some interest. She would lick a grape or feed her dolls a blueberry, which was progress in terms of her aversion to anything in that bowl. I persevered and slowly, one food at a time, she would try a piece. I rarely commented and allowed her to go at her own pace, playing games with her sister of "how many grapes are in the bowl" or "let's eat all the red fruits first". It was as if she saw she was missing out and began to "play" with us.

She now eats everything and anything, and if we dare put pepper on her scrambled eggs, she moans that they are "spicy" (oh, how her taste buds have changed!).

◆ ◆ ◆

Another of our children started off weak and sickly, and went from not knowing what to do with solid food to eating anything you put in front of her – and I mean anything. She was a good eater, and adventurous. I remember other mums commenting that, as a toddler, she loved olives and sun-dried tomatoes and feta cheese and all the things most other kids would turn their noses up at. In my naïvety, I thought this was great, until I learned more about how children with developmental trauma and early food-related issues can use food as a form of comfort. I guess this is hard for a biological parent to comprehend, and I've often had comments like, "Oh, my kid does that as well." But as time went on and my education continued, I knew this was a deeper issue than being a "good eater".

As the kids got older, all of them loved being part of the kitchen and food routines. These moments are treasured in the chaos that is family life. My mum would often have us with her in the kitchen and, although baking wasn't her forte (and certainly isn't mine either), we can both knock up a mean beef stew or roast leg of lamb, and cater for groups of people for barbeques, dinners and playdates. I encouraged (i.e. made) the kids help me with chopping vegetables and food preparation. I quickly worked out that a punnet of mushrooms and a plastic knife were a cheap and easy hour of sensory play for the kids, and I could use the misshapen pieces of vegetable for dinner.

This child of mine who is a "good eater" relished time in the kitchen. She would take a keen interest in certain tasks, like grating cheese, for example. When she was helping out, if I looked out of the corner of my eye I would see her stuffing cheese in her mouth. The first few times I saw her do it, I would give a standard mum answer:

"Darling, no more cheese, you're getting your dinner in a minute." At which, she would turn and deny the cheese stuffing – even with a cheek full of grated cheddar!

Lying about food is likely to make your blood boil, as it did mine. This strange food behaviour continued in different guises. If she was top-and-tailing green beans and thought no one was looking, she'd stuff a few of the brown, curly end bits in her mouth. If she was peeling a potato, she would nibble on a piece of raw potato skin. I found this bizarre and hard to understand, as she had been home for years. Ignoring it was often the only way I could avoid ranting.

Often it was the manipulation and slyness around food that frustrated me. She would say to her little sister, "Do you want me to take your plate to the dishwasher?" My alarm bells would ring, but I would try and give her the benefit of the doubt that maybe, just this once, she was being genuine. She would lift the plate, empty apart from a peanut-sized piece of chewed potato, and as she turned towards the dishwasher, she would shove it into her mouth. It's been chewed, spat out, and it's the size of a peanut!

Most meal times, during her low days or months when self-regulation became hard, we would see her eating like some sort of animal that had been starved for days. She would turn her head as she ate, checking the pot and peering into the oven to make sure there was more left. Her goal was to finish before everyone else, so she could have more. We tried the standard line – "There is loads in the pot, no one is going to steal it, stop acting like a vulture" – but nothing got through. This child ate way more calories a day than either me or my husband, so she wasn't "hungry".

I thought back to mealtimes with her as a younger child. She would stuff food in until she got the dreaded hamster cheeks. She would chew for so long that I would have gagged if I were asked to swallow it. She had been home for nearly a decade, and issues around food and impulse control continued to recur.

One day, after years of education and training and with some new tactics up my sleeve, I tried a different approach. When she started to scavenge for food, I simply said: "I wonder, when you were in the orphanage as a baby, if you had a feeling in your tummy that you knew meant you were hungry. You were so tiny and little that you couldn't speak, so you had to wait until the next milk bottle came round. You were so small you couldn't drink much, so you probably had this feeling that you now know is hunger. I wonder if, when you see food now, you get that feeling back again and maybe your brain tells you that you don't ever want to have that feeling again, and that's why you sometimes eat like you do?"

Absolute silence! It was one of my most emotional parenting moments, where so many of the problems I've had with this girl over the last decade suddenly made sense, and it was all over something so small. She looked up at me, as the nine-year-old little girl she was, and I saw the baby in her. Her eyes welled up and she said, "I think you're right, mummy." I had put words to a feeling she couldn't explain and, to this day, she has never again regressed to these food issues.

She remains a great eater and generally eats a lot (sometimes too much), but she's learned self-control. If someone had placed a tray of donuts in front of her a few years ago, she would have demolished the lot and thrown up afterwards. Now, she will take one. She might ask for another one, and I often say, "It's your choice. Have a think about if you need another one, and if you think you do, then that's your decision to make." Inside, I'm crawling at the thought of her picking up another few and eating until she's sick, but nine times out of ten, she smiles and says, "I think I've had enough," or "I don't think I really need any more."

This tool of self-control has got to be one of my favourite life lessons in my decade of parenting. I feel like it allows the child to take responsibility for their choices and actions – an extremely difficult thing for our adopted children to accomplish, and so satisfying and emotional when you see them master it (even if temporarily).

◆ ◆ ◆

Kids with food issues often have a sideline issue of gross table manners.

One of our kids had manners that frustrated everyone around the table, even years after joining our family. It gets tiring and takes the shine off a family meal to have to continuously nag a child to chew with their mouth closed, to finish eating before talking, to not clang their teeth with the cutlery every time they take a bite, to not grab seconds before anyone else has even finished their first serving.

There is no cure for this one beyond working on the food issues and continually guiding your child about their manners. Now and then, we'll have "pirate night". It's an idea I must have found on the Internet years ago: we have something messy for dinner, sometimes putting a picnic blanket on the floor, and the kids eat like pirates. There is no level of grossness I will so much as raise an eyebrow at. It's a great release of pressure, and all of the kids love it.

◆　◆　◆

If you have a food-obsessed child, there are some areas to focus on in the short-term:

◈ As per our advice on other topics, focus first and foremost on attachment. From a food perspective, that means immediately showing them that you can be relied upon for regular and comforting food, as well as sweet treats. You want your child to feel good when you're feeding them. If they're young enough, feed them yourself, popping little bits of lovely things into their mouths.

◈ If they want to eat more food, give it to them. They need to learn when they are full, and sometimes experience is the best teacher.

◈ Try to get their meal and snack times fairly consistent. You want to create structure and routine for them.

◈ Never, ever, even *think* of leaving the house without food in your bag. Sometimes it's just what you need to stave off a full-blown meltdown.

◈ Of course, get to know your child's likes and dislikes, and try to cater to them to a sensible extent. Don't try to convert them to your family's way of eating immediately; imagine what you would feel like, if that were you?

◈ Encourage slow enjoyment of food. This one will likely take years. Sit at a table, talk, create a nice environment to show them that food can also be social.

◈ Promote sharing – always asking if someone else would like some of what you have. This is really hard when you're worried that someone will take away all of your food. Encourage reciprocity when your child does this for another.

◈ Require that your child ask if they can have something, rather than just helping themselves to the contents of the refrigerator and cupboards. This ensures that they aren't hoarding and also discourages stealing, while allowing you to see what they are eating.

◈ Try not to make food a battleground, especially not right away.

◈ If your child has unhealthy food tendencies, try the "I Wonder" strategy. It is extremely likely that they do not know why they behave the way they do around food. Naming and explaining it can work wonders on their understanding, and then their ability to circuit-break the behaviour.

The Boy Who Never Stops Talking and His Friend, the Boy Who Never Stops Cartwheeling

We have some kids who are jangly. Jangly is far from a technical term, but many of you will understand – it's the child who some days pushes every single button and has you on the edge of a headache, tears or an angry outburst all day. It's so unrelenting, it can feel like your child is trying to get a rise out of you. But while their behaviour might drive you bonkers, especially when they're bored or particularly energetic, it's not usually intentional.

When it comes to my jangly child, I am conscious that our relationship is about 80% positive and 20% "bitch eating crackers".[21]

---

21 If you're not *au fait* with this term, it's when someone can't do anything right in your eyes. Even if they were just sitting eating crackers, you'd be annoyed.

I try so very hard to remain patient and positive in those 20% periods. It takes every ounce of my reserve, and leaves me with no spare capacity for other thoughts or people – including my other children.

During these 20% times, from the moment he wakes until the moment he sleeps, he will tell us every single thought in his head, leaving no "airtime" (as we call it) for anyone else to speak – let alone think.

Or he might attach to a couple of lines from a song and sing it at full volume again and again and again for a couple of weeks. The most memorable one was "I like to move it, move it".

I like to move it, move it. Having a shower.

I like to move it, move it. Eating breakfast.

I like to move it, move it. Walking all the way to school.

I like to move it, move it. Walking all the way home from school.

I like to move it, move it. Setting the table.

I like to move it, move it. Eating dinner.

I like to move it, move it. Watching TV.

Sometimes I take him swimming just so I can't hear him sing for a few blissful seconds.

In his 20% times, he'll inflict similar low-level irritation on his siblings. Then, after a day of all this, he'll sit at the table and chew his dinner with his mouth wide open, with lots of lip-smacking and noise and aimless chatter. This has me fantasising about getting in the car and driving off, never looking back.

Eventually my cup will run over and, after much gentle encouragement to take a break from talking sometimes, I end up telling him that his behaviour is annoying everyone. And that my patience is low. The trouble is, it's hard to explain to him exactly what the issue is – it's just how he's hard-wired.

◆ ◆ ◆

Another one of our kids has almost the same affliction, but instead of talking incessantly, he never stops moving. Literally *never*. From the moment he wakes, he's running, jumping, skipping, clapping, climbing. Even when he's asleep, he writhes and wriggles and wiggles.

This constant need for physical feedback is not an issue on those days when we're at home and he can happily head outside and ride bikes, swing in trees and run around for hours. But some days, this isn't an option. At school, he never stops moving; in class, he's touching, jumping, wriggling. In the car on the way to school, he is touching his siblings, the window, jiggling his legs, clicking his fingers...

On his first day at a new school, I picked him up and checked in with the teacher. She had a beaming smile as she reported back that he was so happy in class, he'd cartwheeled around the playground for both the entire recess and lunch breaks. I smiled wearily, knowing this cartwheeling she found cute and effusive would have her worn out in short order.

We love our cartwheeling boy. But it is hard to be a cartwheeling boy in the modern world...

◆ ◆ ◆

So, what to do when you've a child who pushes your buttons with their incessant talking or moving?

◊ Understand that it's very much to do with their brain development, and very little to do with wanting to annoy people or be disruptive. Much of the chatter is so they don't have free space in their head to think bad thoughts or feel bad feelings. Constant talkers often don't like where their brain goes when they are quiet.

◊ We generally believe constant movers need an unusually high level of sensory feedback because of how their brains have developed in infancy and toddlerhood.

◊ Use a calmer moment to describe to them the behaviour that can frustrate people. Explain to them why they should care: for example, I tell our jangly kid that there are six people in our family and sometimes he takes up all the airtime when someone else would like a turn to speak.

◇ Then, try to give them some practical strategies for dealing with
   that behaviour. If your child is especially chatty, sit with them and
   practice having him tell you every third thought, instead of every
   single one. Praise this behaviour, tell your child how it makes you
   happier to listen and more engaged, and ask them how it feels for
   them.

◇ Understand the value of movement. Instead of thinking of your
   child as a fidgety kid who cannot sit still to save her life, think of
   her as using fidgeting as a way of trying to stay calm when she
   cannot move, for example at a desk at school. There is a reason
   for that fidgeting, and it *is* helping them (though it's unlikely to be
   helping their teacher). Movement is a valuable way to reconnect
   mind and body, and patterned repetitive movement is soothing
   to the limbic (emotional) system. Think about why you rock
   a baby or pat it in a rhythmic manner. As well as being cardio
   exercise, movement is a great calming tool for your child. Try
   letting her have a bit of skateboard time before school. Walk to
   school. Do some skipping in between homework questions. Try
   learning times tables while bouncing a ball against the wall or to
   you. Swimming is good as is running. Find and join a local drum
   circle and go with her, and have fun and relaxation time together.

◇ If your child is wriggly, teach them some methods they can use
   where they are wriggling in a way that doesn't disturb or annoy
   others. Maybe they can wriggle their fingers in their other hand,
   or their toes gently inside their shoes. Maybe they can clench
   and unclench one butt cheek after another, or tighten and release
   their stomach muscles.

◇ If you get mad – and oh, you will – direct it at the behaviour, not
   the child: "This constant beat-boxing in the car is frustrating and
   I'm finding it hard to concentrate on driving." Try not to get to,
   "You are so annoying! Stop! Stop! Stop!" I may once or twice or
   two hundred times have said the latter, but it's an easy change
   around semantics that preserves your child's self-esteem. I try
   hard to do this. If I ever mess it up, I will apologise and reframe
   my annoyance as being directed at the behaviour, not the child.

◈ Look for opportunities to take some pressure off.

   ◇ If you're struggling with volume control, when you are somewhere with no one around – say an empty beach or in the forest – tell your child to shout the place down! Sing the song as loud as they can, shout as loud as they can, because here it doesn't disturb anyone.

   ◇ If it's movement, try getting them moving before they go to school. Once they're ready, blast some music and have them dance like wild people! Or try exercise before school, like running, walking, surfing or swimming.

◈ Help your child to find other ways of calming themselves down without you there. If you feel annoyed, you can be sure other people in their lives are getting annoyed, too. A school teacher with a class of twenty other kids will have less motivation, time and focus to try to improve the behaviour. When you've determined some methods that work for your child, chat to the teacher about them and ask that they encourage your child to use them. For a few weeks, check in with your child often to find out if they are using the strategies to try and cement them.

◈ As a parent, it's helpful to develop a couple of quick calming strategies that don't require equipment. When we used to fly a lot, I would exercise my boy to calm him before boarding, in transit and in immigration queues. I'd hold his hands and he'd jump up and down on the spot, fast and slow, one leg then the other.

◈ In addition to your quick-fix strategies, you'll develop an understanding of the activities that make your child happy and content. For some, it's physical exercise, being in the water, riding a bike, wrestling or kneading bread dough. Some kids can calm themselves through escaping into a movie or a book. Some kids melt when you stroke their arms or rub their backs when they're agitated.

◈ Know yourself in terms of stressful situations where you'll react badly. For me, shopping with kids and packing a bag to go for a swim are hard. I rarely shop with the kids and if I do, I'll take as few as possible. I also keep a wicker bag packed with swimming essentials, including a plastic Ziploc bag full of every pair of swimming goggles we have ever owned.

◈ Take care of yourself in all the ways we describe in the Parental Self-Care section, to try to bring your best self to this tough job. Can you escape for a twenty-minute run? You're likely to return with much-improved perspective.

I take a weird grain of comfort from the fact that when I'm an old lady, I will sit with my jangly child and discuss my day, stream-of-consciousness style. *And then, Emily said to me, what is your favourite daytime TV show? And I said…*

Pee, Wee, Wizz

I t's standard-issue parenthood to get used to the acrid smell of urine. Nappies, toilet-training accidents, bedwetting. What's perhaps less standard about adoptive parenthood is how long pee persists, and how it can be used as a weapon of sorts by your kids.

◆ ◆ ◆

Some of our kids, in their earliest days home, would use wee as a weapon. Toddlers who were adjusting to a new language and didn't quite have the words to express themselves would show us how they were feeling by peeing their pants, or taking their pants off to pee on the lounge room floor.

There's not a lot you can do about this – their choice of expression is limited, and as their language and attachment improves, this will likely stop being an issue. If they're old enough, I'd make them clean it up and tell them that it's better to get your anger out in different ways, and direct them with some ideas on how to do that.

◆ ◆ ◆

We were renovating the bathrooms in our house. It was long overdue, and we finally had the funds to do it – replacing orange tiles and scratched wooden vanities with beautiful hexagonal tiles and grey-

and-white vanities. We were up to the upstairs bathroom, which meant that the kids sleeping upstairs now had to trundle downstairs when they needed to go – no mean feat in the middle of the night, busting to wee and eyes and head blurry with dreams of dragons and adventures.

This man-child of mine had started out strong: toilet training a little after two years old, and then just wearing nappies at night. The problem was that he never stopped: the nappies at night were a feature of his bedtime routine until late primary school. We tried a range of methods, googled for more ideas but, after years of trial and error, we had gotten absolutely nowhere.

It started to become an issue for our boy when friends began to speak excitedly about sleepovers. I hoped this might be the encouragement he needed to stop wearing night nappies, as I wasn't sending him off with a nappy in his bag for a sleepover with a child who probably hadn't worn a nappy for five years.

Around this time, he just announced he was done with nappies at night and was no longer going to wet the bed. He'd just decided enough was enough. Um, OK – it looked like here was the self-motivation I'd been wishing for. And he was working hard to show that he was really, truly done.

Fast forward a week, and my husband kept complaining that his room smelt like pee. He confessed that, yes, he'd wet the bed. We stripped the bed sheets, washed his pajamas. We never shouted or got angry: we had realised the futility of that years ago, and knew that it made no difference whatsoever.

But the smell persisted. We put the floor rug outside for some sun. Still no improvement.

The next day, searching for the pee-sodden clothes or pee-sodden something that was causing the smell, we unearthed the problem: a huge black patch, underneath a couple of toy boxes and well hidden. Instead of going downstairs to pee, he had simply peed right on the floor, in the corner of the room.

He knew this was absolutely unacceptable and, to pre-adoption me, the whole scenario would have seemed simply unthinkable. He had deliberately chosen to pee on the floor and then omitted to tell us every time we asked, over the course of several days, why his room smelt like pee. Sadly, by this stage in our parenting journey, neither of us were at all surprised.

He was dealt out a consequence based on his action: spending hours over the next few days sandpapering the blackened patch (this was purely to drive home the lesson we were teaching him; we had to get a professional sander in to come and fix the floor properly).

This isn't a story I tell my "normal" friends, as I'd worry they'd label my boy weird. But my adoptive mum friends understand this one, and know that there are perhaps a dozen other pee-related stories I could tell them, too. At least, I suppose, it's not poo – an issue for many attachment-challenged kids. Dodged a bullet with that one, I guess.

◆ ◆ ◆

So how do you deal with pee issues?

◊ Firstly, ensure there are no underlying medical issues. One of our kids had a urinary tract infection and we were able to treat it easily with cranberry essence probiotics.

◊ We felt our boy's pee issues were physical rather than psychological and, given this, we decided to simply give it time. When he wet his bed, we'd never show anger or disappointment (only if he hid it from us or lied about it). Instead, we were very matter-of-fact. He'd strip his bed and I'd help him put the sheets in the washing machine. We bought a couple of special sheets to go over the fitted sheet that protected the mattress a little. We let him wear night nappies even as he got older and was close to needing elderly incontinence pants, as the night nappies weren't going to fit any more.

◊ When he didn't wet the bed, which was infrequent, we would praise him and celebrate the effort. We did try sticker/reward charts, but they just set him up for failure as he didn't last long before wetting the bed again. So we took small steps, and waited for him to really want to stop.

◈ I've already mentioned that his friends were starting to have sleepovers. Then, there was his first overnight school camp. Together, we worked on his bedwetting and while we knew he really, in fact desperately, wanted to be able to stay over with a friend as well as go to camp, he still couldn't get his bedwetting under control.

◈ We finally went to the doctors and found there was a nasal spray that he could use when he was having a night away that would stop the pee. We tried it out a couple of times and it worked a treat. I wasn't keen to overuse it, but it enabled him to go to camp and to a friend's birthday party.

◈ Over time, though, as he calmed down more and grew older, he just stopped. We could have railed against the years of bedwetting, but I'm glad we didn't make him feel shame – we relaxed and let him be ready. And slowly, slowly, slowly, but surely, he got there all on his own.

Learning Challenges

All of our kids have different challenges with learning. If you've read the earlier chapter about the impact of trauma on the brain, you won't be surprised by this.

Early on, we used to try and spend time solving the learning issues. We've since learned that we need to work on helping the kids' brains catch up to where they "should" be, before trying to push academic challenges onto them. We try, of course, but we spend more of our time and attention ensuring they will be receptive to learning first.

You've read the trauma introduction, you've lived with your child, you understand the issues.

In many of the privileged school communities we've belonged to, the general understanding of children with trauma is extremely low. We have put together a downloadable booklet that you can provide to your child's teachers and school.[22] The best teachers, counsellors and principals have invariably been keen to learn and understand our children, and pleased to partner with us and implement at school the same strategies we use at home.

◆　◆　◆

---

22 www.lionheartfamilies.com/resources

Some advice on working with your child's school:

◈ Talk to your school. Maybe have a round-table with your psychologist and the teachers. Most teachers welcome parents giving them a heads-up on what to expect in class. Depending on the level of behavioural issues, you could have an informal chat with the teacher about your child's developmental learning and what you have gleaned from your experience. In complex cases, you could have a full meeting with all interested parties and develop an action plan for the child at school.

◈ Some things that may help teachers to know about children with trauma:

　◇ Why they can be impulsive. Without an understanding of trauma, it would be easy to categorise your child as naughty. You can help them reframe their thinking, from *what is wrong with you* to *what happened to you?* This might help the teacher to rethink a child's behaviour as being a challenge to their authority. It might help them view the child's lack of self-regulation as the source of their impulsiveness and lack of attentiveness.

　◇ You can explain why your child might not be learning very easily – they are spending so much energy in a highly sensitive and agitated state that less learning information is received by the higher brain functions, and even less is remembered. This explains why a teacher (and a parent) might have to repeat facts many more times than they would for other children. It also explains why a child with trauma can cognitively understand, for example, a maths technique, but five minutes later it is like the memory has been wiped.

　◇ Putting the child at the front of the class might make things worse if the child feels in danger if there are people behind them. Suggest putting them to the side instead.

　◇ You child's sensory integration issues may help explain why they are fidgeting in class and are unable to sit still. They are craving sensory input, and the teacher needs to expect and

understand the swinging legs, rocking on c
their mouth, and chewing things. These th
for the child's central nervous system. Sit
moving is probably impossible for them,
force them to do so will increase their agitation. This is
challenge to the teacher's authority.

◇ This might also explain why the child always seems to be in
trouble in the playground. Your child may sense danger where
others do not, and react accordingly. Their "normal play" is
everyone else's "rough play" due to their reduced capacity to
feel tactile input.

◇ Traumatised children have low self-esteem and need as much
praise as possible, like a much younger child.

◇ Traumatised children often have a highly simplified sense of
fairness and can become very angry if they feel the teacher is
acting unfairly towards them, or has class favourites.

◇ Schools often threaten to remove a child from their sports team
if the child has misbehaved. For a child with a history of trauma,
relational interaction is extremely important, and removing
them from the team is not going to help them. It is unlikely to
have any impact on their impulsivity (because their capacity
for self-regulation is limited), but it *is* likely to affect their self-
esteem, and will mean losing out on the valuable opportunity
to learn from interactions with other children and the coach.

◆ ◆ ◆

A close partnership with schools makes for a much easier life. I have
chats with one of my children's teachers during which we moan
to each other about some of her more challenging behaviours, and
sympathise with each other. We also share strategies on what works
well, and try to ensure consistency between home and school. Build
allegiances with your children's broader support team – you all need
each other.

Request. Repeat. Request. Repeat

"**P**lease put your shoes away, then tidy your room and bring your homework out".

Child brings pencil case, no homework. Shoes still on lounge floor, bedroom still untidy.

"Put your shoes away, then tidy your room and bring your homework book out, please".

Homework book now accompanies pencil case; shoes and room in the same state.

After some more requests, a shoe is put away. Just the one.

"Put your second shoe away, please."

"Thanks, now please tidy up your room."

"Good, now tidy up the floor, please."

"I said, tidy up the floor."

"*Tidy up the floor.*"

You get the picture, and would understand if I turned to alcohol at the end of the day when you hear that this is how the conversation goes every time I need him to do something. *Anything.*

In the early years, this repetition didn't bother me, as I saw it was the same with other children of a similar age. Around school-going age, though, the other kids started to be able to take in more complex sets of instructions, and remember more than just the last thing you said to them.

My experience with children who have faced trauma is that their brains are so chaotic, so disorganised, that it takes many years more for them to be able to calm the internal chaos enough to follow multi-step instructions.

After reading more about brain development and the impact of early trauma on the brain, I better understood and accepted that if I wanted compliance with a request, I needed to ask in a way that would lead to success.

"Put your shoes away please, then come back to me."

"Great job. Please could you put away all of the mess on your floor?"

"Excellent, now please make your bed and come back to me."

"Good job, now can you bring your homework book and pencil out to me?"

A regular frustration for me when it comes to my kids' communication challenges is that it feels like it's all on me. For example, if we're packing our things up to go to the beach, I despatch requests and now know they are unlikely to be fulfilled. Or a request to put a hat on will be complied with, only to be undone after a different request – the hat taken off and left on his bed – so I have to keep a running tally. The mental gymnastics of running parallel lists in my head is exhausting. It's like every "to do" list you've had this year, piled up on top of each other – the things I need to do or remember, and the things I've asked them to do. It requires a lot of vigilance, and sometimes you need to pick your battles.

◆ ◆ ◆

Some short-term strategies to help with this include:

◊ Read the section on Trauma to better understand why your child behaves like this. It will still frustrate you, but you will be more empathetic.

◊ Play word games to help him remember things in sequence, such as "I went to the shop and bought a grapefruit," then the next person repeats the shopping list and adds another item: "I went to the shop and bought a grapefruit and a pair of shoelaces," and so on.

◇ Prioritise activities that promote calm and organisation, such as doing jigsaw puzzles. This particular child never volunteers to do one, but if I promise a movie after we've done one, he'll actually enjoy it.

◇ Teach the child the power of breathing to calm him down. He is too mentally disorganised to get anything out of proper meditation, no matter how short, so I'll count breaths with him: in for four, hold for four, out for eight, and repeat this five times. His wriggles and his mental gymnastics notably calm. It only lasts about five minutes, but I'm hopeful that with maybe twenty years of work, we'll get this humming.

◇ For your own sanity, write lists. When we're packing for a holiday, if I am at home I will often just pack the kids' clothes myself. If I'm busier, I'll write them detailed lists and have them pull everything out, and then check if off with an adult. There is no way I can run that mentally without writing it down – packing for an hour at the beach is hard enough!

Longer-term help may include counselling, wrestle therapy, occupational therapy, and simple mindfulness meditations, all of which help to calm the mind over time.

God speed, sisters and brothers. This one is hard yards, and there are no easy solutions.

Disorganisation: Stuff

I remember vividly one of the first few days I had my girl home. She lined up her little shoes from smallest to biggest. Be still, my beating heart! Her brand new running shoes, little sandals, her dress-up princess heels – all perfectly arranged. I took it as a sign of what was to come.

How wrong I was.

This child of mine, gorgeous in so many ways, is the messiest human I have ever known. Not when it comes to her personal hygiene and grooming – although that takes some prompting and nagging from time to time. But her things and her room are scarily messy.

I had naïvely thought that because she'd had so few possessions for the first few years of her life, she would treasure material things. Instead, apart from that shoe lining-up folly and the early weeks of pure delight at the new clothes in her wardrobe, she has shown that she couldn't care less about things.

While we created a bedroom together that looks lovely on the surface – pictures on the walls, posters tacked up, a pretty rug and bedcover – that's where all notion of beauty stops. Open the wardrobe door and out spills an avalanche of junk. Washed and folded clothes, dirty clothes, apple cores, half-eaten sandwiches in bags, dirty tissues (like *really* dirty tissues), wads of hair from a hairbrush, old toothbrushes with toothpaste still on them.

Originally, we insisted on a clean room each night. Then it became every weekend – it would be a prerequisite to TV or iPad time. Then, every holidays, her Nan or I would go in with her and pull everything out, sort things and throw out all the rotting food, while she "helped".

I have since stopped participating in this monumental waste of time. Cleanliness and tidiness is important to me, and I insist on it in family areas. But I realised, after a few years of trying, that all I was doing was creating work for myself and having zero impact on my child. She'd spend a day cleaning up with me and, instead of feeling great satisfaction from being organised, would on that very same day continue with the habits that had gotten her room to such a treacherous state.

Another one of our children is extremely tidy. She carefully looks after her possessions and pays attention to how things look. She sometimes needs a nag to pick up her clothes and change her bed sheets, but she would never have rotting apples mixed in with her shoes and pencils in the bottom of her wardrobe.

While this challenge is not super removed from the challenges of biological parenting (especially as kids become teenagers), in our experience, comfort with extreme mess is more prevalent with adopted kids. If they struggle with internal organisation because their brains are chaotic, then organisation outside of themselves is nigh-on impossible. The action you should take really depends on your tolerance, and your willingness to add this to your list of things to argue about on a daily basis.

In our opinion, when you're having no impact on the habits of your child and merely creating work for yourself, then let it go if you think you can live with it. Occasionally, when the state of mould gets out of control, I'll stop and yell to clean up the hellhole that is their room and they'll jump up and do it. Because I'm not low-level nagging them about clean rooms on a daily basis, they know I'm serious.

But most days I prefer to focus on love, kindness, a bit of reading and schoolwork. When they're not in them, I tend to shut their bedroom doors so I don't have to bear witness to the filth. And for the child whose room faces the living room, I bought a Frida Kahlo bamboo curtain, which saves my sanity as I can no longer see in from the sofa.

◆ ◆ ◆

It's not just the child's bedroom; lack of care for possessions usually extends to their clothes, their toys, and everyone else's things, too.

Here are just a few examples I could think of from the last few weeks:

◊ One of the kids had a new t-shirt and, despite our warnings, left it on at dinner and got food all over it. It's soaking, but unlikely to be retrievable. This is about the millionth time this has happened.

◊ One of the kids borrowed my sandals to go to the beach. We went to walk up the hill after a long swim, worn out, happy and salty. She jumped and squirmed from the heat on her bare feet. Where are the sandals you had on? Oops, left them at the beach. Not to worry, she says, and keeps walking. I am, after all this time, still gobsmacked by the ease with which she gave up on the shoes, and I made her go back for them. She can't quite believe I made her do this.

◊ One of the kids borrowed my favourite, very wide-brimmed hat for a day out. She left it somewhere during the day and forgot to mention it until weeks later, when I wanted to wear it.

◊ On a weekend away in a rented cottage, one of the kids was playing on the sundeck after we'd had a big walk. She decided carving her name in the wooden railing was an appropriate memorial to our weekend.

These came very easily; there are many, many more. So what to do? We've explained about having to work, that money isn't endless, refused to replace damaged things, made them speak to the cottage owner to confess and apologise. None of these approaches has had much lasting impact.

One thing that has had an impact, though, has been to create an IOU or a bill for them on my phone. I don't do this for each and every damaged thing – that would be a full-time job to administer. But when a child is racking up a few things and not caring enough, they'll get a bill. Nothing will be spent on them in a discretionary sense until the bill is repaid. Say, for example, we're at a café and the kids want to have milkshakes. I'll remind the indebted child of their bill, and ask them to choose to have water instead and take the money I would have spent on their milkshake off the bill. They also have to do extra chores, like washing the car or helping to clean out the garage, and we'll deduct an agreed amount from their bill. This method has worked a treat. One of the kids had an $800 bill once. Yes, that was a bad time.

Lack of Identity

When you first start parenting a child who simply wants to make everyone around her happy, you think how charming she is, and you think what a great job you are doing with the parenting.

Our girl always had plenty of friends amongst her peers, though her attachments to them seemed a little fickle – they always seemed more into her than her into them. She was always happy to replace one with another quickly.

As she got older, and the other kids were becoming more and more assertive, her desire to keep people happy meant she became a target for bullies. Her "friends" would request she share some of her lunch money, with no suggestion of it being reciprocated. We could see it upset her a little, but she struggled to say no to people. Her low self-esteem and unsteady sense of self meant she didn't trust that people would still like her if she didn't comply with them.

We also noticed that when she had a friend to stay, she'd happily chat and engage for a while and then, to our minds, rudely retreat for a bit. After we saw this happen a few times, we started to realise she was not this charming extrovert we'd observed – at least, not all the time.

Eventually it clicked. Children that have been institutionalised beyond the baby stage were one of a number, fighting for cuddles, food and attention, and their only currency was cute compliance or loud crying and moaning. I saw it myself: the cutest kids got the best clothes, their hair done nicely, the nicest place to sleep, the extra plate of food. This was my girl's survival mechanism. She had been smart, and survived on her charm.

We needed to help her keep her innate charm, while working with her to improve her sense of self and her willingness to assert herself. While it's difficult for her, it is vital to ensure she is less vulnerable to exploitation, and less likely to royally mess up friendships through lying to keep the peace.

◆ ◆ ◆

This is a continuing effort, and some of the strategies we are using include:

◈ Understanding where this behaviour comes from, seeking therapy and talking about this behaviour pattern with trusted counsellors. She now intellectually owns this historical pattern as one that worked, and we're working on her acceptance that it's not a viable life pattern.

◈ Assertiveness role-play: she'll tell us about something that happened at school, and we'll take the role of her, and get her to be the other person. We'll model some things she could say. Then she'll have a go.

◈ Watching carefully and giving her boundaries where she can't uphold them by herself. For example, I'll check her lunch money online and if I can see she is buying stuff for other kids, I'll speak with her and she'll skip the next instalment of lunch money. While she might rail against us for our strictness at times, we need to provide her structure. This is hard on us, and annoying. It would be extremely hard to do as a single parent with more than one child; it can be quite an intense job.

◈ Meditation focused on self-love works well to make her feel worthy; to consider herself worthy of happiness, health and peace. I can see her body calm instantly when listening to these words. Using the Calm app on the iPhone, we do five minutes or so most mornings as she's waking up, and many evenings before sleep.

◈ We're slowly building her physical stamina and confidence with martial arts. We want the kids to have the skills and confidence that they might need to look after themselves if things are going wrong. The patterned, repetitive routines are also calming to the central nervous system, while the precise poses help develop a sense of where the body is in space. Sometimes, children with developmental trauma struggle to know where their arms and feet are, and have to look at their feet all the time.

◈ When we assert ourselves in our daily lives, we'll tell the kids about it as we download our day over dinner. We want them to see examples of living, breathing strong people so that they think it's normal.

◈ We talk to the kids and use examples of people liking and respecting each other even when they don't agree on everything. We also explain to them that not everyone will like you, and that's OK.

Two Steps Forward, One Step Back

I have worked with and hustled and hassled and loved and therapied and loved and hugged my children, and together moved them from a bad place to a pretty good one.

And then, I have been devastated to see the child slip back into self-destructive behaviour patterns, or habits they haven't displayed for years and years. It happens unexpectedly, and it takes a while to sift through what's really going on. It also takes a while to move yourself from confusion to denial to acceptance to treatment.

One of my children has always had trouble with authority – an inability to comply with adult demands, with a side of stealing and lying. We worked long and hard on these habits, and it took years. It saw me cancelling his birthday party; it saw him deliberately ruin Christmas, to the extent that my parents took the other children out for a walk as things were so bad at home; it resulted in suspension from preschool (I wish I was joking!), and almost daily requests to visit the principal at primary school for nearly a full school year.

Over a period of many years and through the combination of lots of physical activity, wrestling therapy, consequence-based parenting, love, hugs, professional therapy, neurological assessment, and assurances that we still loved him even when he made a mistake, he slowly worked his way out of it.

We noticed he started to tell us he loved us, after about eight years of parenting him! We noticed he'd sometimes seek out our hugs, and come up to our room in the morning and ask how we'd slept. The calls from school were infrequent; he made friends and interacted with them fairly normally. He was invited to parties, and his friends' parents regularly reported back how well-mannered, polite and cute he was.

It broke my heart to say it, but I told my husband that this was the first time I had genuinely enjoyed being his parent, that I hadn't been "faking it til I made it". The years and years before were merely struggle, with an occasional glimpse of abstract cute.

We lapped up this boy, now our least challenging child – happy with a game of football, a full belly, a funny cartoon on TV and a hug goodnight. He was all of a sudden delightful, and it was such a salve after the hard years we'd had with him. Family and friends commented how much he had calmed down. We started to allow him to go to the occasional sleepover with a friend. He was always full of bravado, assuring me how good a time he'd had and that he hadn't missed me at all.

When some of our oldest friends wondered aloud if he wanted to go with them on their holiday to Legoland to keep their son company, we were now able to entertain the idea. Could it work? Would he listen to someone else for two weeks? Would he miss us? He was keen, and we thought it would be good for him. We had been giving some of the other kids more attention the last year or so, as they'd very much needed it. It would be nice for him to have this opportunity, to enjoy some serious "boy time".

We insisted he first go and stay with my friends for a weekend, so they all had a trial at living together. My friend texted me multiple times that weekend telling me what a dream he was: polite, funny, well-behaved, ate everything they offered him. It was all going to work out just fine. They booked the tickets. He was set to go about six weeks later, and it was all he could talk about.

Then, within a week and out of nowhere, some of his old habits resurfaced. He stole, and lied about it. Disappointed, we threatened to call the trip off, but instead used other consequences. We spoke a lot about trust and our expectations of his behaviour. We almost never use "chances" with this child; they have never worked. Doing so now was unusual for us, but we so wanted him to be able to go and, more importantly, I had paid the airfare already.

A week later, he re-offended, more spectacularly than before and in a way he had to know would be found out. We were incredibly disappointed.

I'd thought he understood, that he realised he was on thin ice and his trip away was very much under threat. After this episode, we could not consider rewarding his behaviour or giving him any more chances. The trip was off.

While he was sheepish about being in trouble again, I was surprised that he didn't appear too disappointed. In fact, after observing him for a day or so, I felt like he seemed relieved to not be allowed to go. As the emotion drained out of it, we spoke more about his actions and he confirmed our suspicions.

A large part of him really wanted to go, but he self-sabotaged as his deep-seated fear of abandonment overrode the potential fun. How had I not anticipated this?! I'd wanted to believe he was past that, but these events reminded me that his fears ran deep and could come up at any time, no matter how settled and secure he seemed. I wish I'd anticipated this earlier – it cost me a lot of money.

I tell this story to illustrate that while it is frustrating when a child reverts to old destructive behaviours, there is usually an underlying reason that is helpful to uncover. Once you have, you can use the "I Wonder" strategy that we reference in the Therapy Toolbox section and, if still needed, the behavioural management tools you used to deal with the behaviour the first time around.

I Give Up

If your child is frequently out of control, possibly violent, destroying the rest of your family relationships, alienating your wider family, your friends and your community, with no prospect of change, it is natural to start to think that perhaps you are not the right parent for this child, or that you cannot give them the help they need and someone else would be better at it.

If there are other children in the family, you will be concerned about ensuring that they also have a childhood that isn't filled with angst, fear and violence. Or you may recognise the stress is straining your relationships to breaking point. Why continue when the child does not show the slightest bit of affection or attachment, and seems intent on destroying everything and every relationship?

Having knowledge about trauma is a good start to understanding behaviour, and can replace anger and frustration with understanding and frustration – a key difference!

Even so, I have had several days through the years where I'll throw my hands up and feel utterly bereft, thinking *I give up* on the hopes and dreams I have of raising my adopted kids to be OK.

We have become very tough over the course of our adoptive parenting decade. We are adept at school suspensions, expulsion, police visits, stealing, lying, worrying sexual behaviour and occasional violence. At times, that's all in a day's work. Feeling hopeless is never a knee-jerk reaction, and it comes neither easily nor quickly.

But now and again, there will be a catastrophe that feels like a spotlight shining on how awful we are as parents, how hopeless our intensive efforts are, how much heartache and angst we are exposing the rest of the family to. And we feel fed up, used and abused. We pour our heart, soul, time and money into helping heal a child, and they self-sabotage or self-destruct and seem to care very little about it.

We look ahead to decades of problems and are fearful. I feel jealous of people who have conventional families, and whose problems (from the outside at least) seem no more serious than a C on a report card.

On these hopeless days, you can feel so desperate that you begin to research boarding schools. We have worried about whether they would end up in jail – that is, if they managed to escape juvenile detention – or, failing that, end up a drug-addicted prostitute, so poor was their impulse control and so strong their risk-seeking behaviour.

These feelings are hard to speak about (remember, we are supposed to be Mother Teresa), but they are where you can end up when things seem hopeless.

I have felt so depressed about our choices and our family's future that all I wanted to do was escape. I remember driving fast on a highway, alone one morning after dropping the kids at school, and thinking that all I had to do was swing the wheel too far to the left and all this would go away.

I have fantasised about having a minor car accident, in which no one was seriously hurt, but where I was required to recuperate alone in a quiet hospital for a week.

Our family challenges have twice resulted in me becoming depressed and getting counselling and medication.

I have been so fraught that I drank half a bottle of whisky late one night and took myself off to the beach. (Thankfully, a possum scared the bejesus out of me and I scurried home before I'd made it 100 metres.)

None of these feelings are evident on the surface. We love these kids as hard as anyone can love their kids. These are the 1am conversations between exhausted and hopeless parents. These are the reasons that when I see rare media coverage of an adoptive parent sending her child back to Russia or wherever, I do not judge. I think, poor family, poor parents, poor kid, I wish they had gotten the help they needed.

We've had these dark days a few times, and we have survived. We still have all our kids and some of our sanity. It is natural to get burnt out and feel like you are wasting your time and energy, your *life*, on a totally ungrateful, hateful child. You keep giving and giving and get nothing in return, except angst, grief, insults and perhaps violence. Why would anyone want to persist with that when it is destroying everything you hold dear?

◆ ◆ ◆

When you feel like you can't go on parenting your adopted kids and are desperate, here are some things that have worked for us:

◊ Let yourself talk through all of the options, no matter how crazy, with your partner or a trusted friend. Don't make it taboo. When we do this, we are getting our frustrations out and imagining a different life, but the process always leads us to the sensible conclusion that we think we'll be OK, like we have always been.

◊ Keep these conversations between you and your partner, or your adoptive parent friends. Before I was in the thick of adoptive parenting, I would have harshly judged a parent confessing these feelings. I've heard adoptive parents say that if they complain about their child at all, family and friends will say, "Well, this is what you asked for."

◊ Take the long view: things *will* probably work out. Trust your experience (or even ours) that in days, weeks or years from now, this moment is likely to be a distant memory. We have seen children go from extremely damaged and traumatised to well-functioning. Trust in time.

◊ Get some perspective. Distract yourself with a stupid movie or Candy Crush to give your brain a break. Call in reinforcements if you have some, and get out for an hour or two.

◊   Accept that self-care is vital, each and every day. Do not wait
    until you are in a crisis. Use some of the techniques in the Self-
    Care section.

◊   Please, please, please don't talk with the kids about this. It is hard
    not to throw barbs when you are tired, angry and desperate, and
    want to show your child you are at the end of your tether and that
    they need to change. They need to see unconditional love from
    you. You know all this.

The exception to the comments above around taking the long view is
if one child is putting another child in physical danger. That would be
a different conversation entirely, and requires professional help and
advice. I fundamentally believe that you cannot allow the problems
of one child to destroy the lives of the rest of the family – that is our
line in the sand. But often, there are many options beyond "I give up."

Therapy & Strategy Toolbox

———◇———

"Courage doesn't always roar. Sometimes courage is the quiet voice at the end of the day saying, 'I will try again tomorrow.'"

Mary Anne Radmacher

———◇———

Section Contents

Introduction

Between our three families, there aren't many therapies we haven't tried over the last decade. Child counselling, parent counselling, family counselling, positive parenting, therapeutic parenting, psychiatric intervention, occupational therapy, speech therapy, kinesiology, learning therapy – you name it, we've tried it.

We've found that a lot of therapies work well and support the work we do at home for our kids. We list many of these in this chapter.

We have also had lots of therapies that proved to be an absolute waste of time and money. We are seriously skeptical about the "professional" therapy we've received over the years. Without specialist adoption training or trauma awareness, otherwise competent professionals can be fairly ineffective.

In our early days, we sought help for the issues we could see. We had speech therapy for a child who had formed a strange speech habit. We had occupational therapy in the early days, for muscle tone and strength, to counteract the months our child spent lying in a cot. These helped a little, but we've since realised that working on healing the inner trauma in these children was never addressed, and we now know that this should be the initial focus.

Any therapist you are working with needs to have experience with children who have been through trauma. This is crucial: we had many false starts with therapists who knew less about trauma than we did.

I remember being at the end of my tether a few years ago when I was describing to a clinical psychologist some worrying symptoms in my eight year old. These included licking the walls, pressing her cheek against light switches and shuffling along the floor like a centipede, as well as some behaviours that would surface right before bed (like pulling at her eyelashes or at her hair on her arms). When I tried to explain all this, I could see the woman looking at me like I had completely lost the plot. After an hour of me pouring my heart out, having a good cry and being charged $150, she suggested I leave the light on at night and do a lifebook for her (like I hadn't already tried these things).

A friend of ours saw a psychologist who said she didn't want to know about the child's early years as "that wasn't the issue now". If you are seeing someone like this with an adopted child, run a mile.

In fact, our dissatisfaction with the general level of knowledge around children and trauma has seen two of us study this topic in recent years. Selina has completed an MSc in Psychology, and had further training in Dyadic Developmental Psychotherapy with a specialty in adoption. Rob has started studying towards a Graduate Certificate in Child Developmental Trauma.

Our advice around therapies is to figure out what your core strategies are going to be, and experiment a little around the edges. Core strategies will tend to involve counsellors and psychologists, sometimes psychiatrists.

After these, our use of other professionals ebbs and flows depending on what's happening with our family. Some of our kids have used occupational and speech therapists to help with different issues. Sometimes they've been great; sometimes it hasn't moved the dial at all.

One of the challenges with these add-on, shorter-term therapies has been leaving the therapists' offices with a page-long list of things to do. It can feel overwhelming to add this list to an already long list of parenting responsibilities. We try to do them, but over time we've learned to take the one or two we think will be most effective and focus on those. We also have taken on the highlights from the different therapists' advice and incorporated these into our regular routines, with great success. Take what works, and be intuitive enough with your child to leave behind what doesn't, without guilt.

Finally, we use some therapies that are not really "therapies" but rather things that work for our families. These are far easier to introduce into your lives and might make all the difference, relatively simply and often cheaply. These are gold, and we're excited to share some of them with you.

Psychologists and Psychiatrists

Most psychologists and psychiatrists are good people with a genuine desire to help. Unfortunately, this alone is not enough to be effective. There are people who know what they are doing when it comes to children with trauma, and there is everyone else. In my opinion, having a psychologist with experience, who understands what your family and your child are going through, is critical to achieving any kind of top-down therapy. If you see a professional in this space and it doesn't feel right, keep looking. A lot of psychologists deal with the more common issues of anxiety, depression and so on; trauma is quite a specialised field, and child trauma even more so.

A good psychologist will be a collaborator and a strategic partner, not a director. You may have to go through several psychologists before you find one with whom you can develop a rapport, and who understands the kind of trauma that your child is living with. Get yourself a psychologist who you can have a decent relationship with.

Some parents I have met over the years hope to outsource the psychological welfare of their child to a psychologist. This is very tempting, of course: send the child to therapy once a week and, *voila*, in a year or two the child will be better! It is wishful thinking to believe that a one-hour session is going to do anything other than provide time for discussion and reflection, and perhaps a bit of realisation. The real growth or resolution happens at home, with you.

This means that *you* need to be the expert on your child, thinking about their behaviour, motivations, friends and relationships, what works, what doesn't, what might work, what you have read about and want to discuss, etc. Think of psychologists and psychiatrists as facilitators – making it easier for your child to recover from their trauma, and for you to help them while staying sane yourself and keeping your family together.

Psychiatrists are a very different story: I think of them as specialist pharmacological resources rather than a source of practical help. They generally think through the lens of pharmacology, and this is not always a bad thing.

Our view is that psycho-pharmacology is good, within limits. Understand what drugs can and cannot do for your child. They cannot overcome trauma, but they can help stabilise a dysregulated child who cannot sleep or who is so hyperactive that any little thing tips them over the edge. Drugs can help empty a bit of stress from the overflowing cup, to give your child a chance to relax and inhabit their bodies without rage. Then, when something stressful happens, there is a bit of capacity left for the child to deal with it without getting overwhelmed. But don't think of drugs as a cure. They are an aid. You still need to do the work to get your child to feel safe in their body and in their habitat, otherwise when you stop the drugs, nothing will have changed.

◆   ◆   ◆

Our general rhythm with psychologists and psychiatrists has taken a while to develop.

We regularly see our family counsellor (a psychologist experienced with kids who've suffered trauma), and have done for almost seven years. When everyone is stable, we'll see her every couple of months. This is frequent enough that she stays familiar. Even if she just chats with the kids about school and there are no harder topics discussed, these "in between" sessions are crucial as they mean she's able to really help our kids when they need it.

From time to time, she'll also step back and say to us: you guys are really doing a great job, look how far the kids have come! And some days, that is all you need to hear.

When times are tough, we'll increase the frequency of our visits and focus on the specific issue and child intensively. The effectiveness of this is improved markedly because of the maintenance visits in between: she is a trusted adult, and she knows the kids well.

There is some evidence that suggests that the efficacy of any particular cognitive therapy is a function of the relationship between the therapist and the child, and it matters less whether it is a talking therapy or art therapy, play therapy, etc. I would not put occupational therapy into this category, however.

We've seen a psychiatrist for some of our kids only when they needed the help of medication. When this need no longer exists, we don't do maintenance visits, provided we remain on the patient list and can return at short notice.

Another permanent add-on for us is the school counsellor. Again, a pre-emptive approach will be more effective. Build a relationship with the counsellor yourself, so they see you as a partner and will pick up the phone sooner rather than later. We've seen some fairly average ones in terms of their experience with trauma, and some amazing ones. Given that you can't choose the school counsellor, you need to get them on side.

Counselling is used on an ongoing basis for all of our families.

The "I Wonder" Strategy

One of the most ineffective adoptive parenting things that many of us do is to see a troubling behaviour and ask our child, *why?*

The child (genuinely) has no idea why. You get mad that they don't know, and you feel like they are trying to annoy you more. Your anger increases, they retreat into themselves, and everyone is in a worse place.

Selina shared a strategy that she learned during her developmental psychotherapy training in London. We've all been trying this strategy since, and we're now huge advocates of it. We call it the "I Wonder" strategy.

Some behaviour is so ingrained, and the kids don't understand for a second why they do some of the things they do. Their reasons might relate to events very early in their childhood that they can't even remember. The "I Wonder" strategy is basically asking hypothetical questions and trying to frame certain behaviours.

This therapy is quite controversial and relies on empathy, not reassurance. The "I Wonder" approach works with kids who can't understand their actions and behaviours, and whose logical reasoning brain is less developed.

When one of the kids is having an issue or behaving badly, and it is a situation that continues over time, it's worth trying to help the kids to understand why they are behaving that way. We spoke in the chapter titled "Mum, I'm Hungry, Hungry, Hungry" about how we used this with a child who was always hungry.

Instead of getting exasperated with her, we asked her: "I wonder, when you were in the orphanage as a baby, if you had a feeling in your tummy that you knew meant you were hungry. You were so tiny and little that you couldn't speak, so you had to wait until the next milk bottle came round. You were so small you couldn't drink much, so you probably had this feeling that you now know is hunger. I wonder if, when you see food now, you get that feeling back again and maybe your brain tells you that you don't ever want to have that feeling again, and that's why you sometimes eat like you do?"

If a child is constantly chattering in a meaningless way, you could try the "I Wonder" approach: "I wonder if you are talking all the time because you don't want to think?" The child may realise this is true, and then be able to tell you that silence is hard for them. Silences make them remember times or events that are not positive, so chatting or mumbling away is a way out.

Since Selina shared this strategy, we are all using it and helping our kids gain greater insight into their behaviour.

Therapeutic Parenting

Dan Hughes has written a great book about therapeutic parenting that I highly recommend.[23] The essence of therapeutic parenting is that parents control the manner in which the child interacts with the outside world, because the child cannot regulate themselves sufficiently to handle that kind of interaction.

Therapeutic parenting takes away a lot of the stress of trying to get a child to do what they are told. Take this simple scenario: *Your dirty clothes are all over the floor, why can't you put them in the washing basket? I am sick and tired of picking them up. Have you picked them up yet?* The same thing happens the next day.

With therapeutic parenting, this scenario becomes: *If you put your clothes in the washing basket, I will be happy to wash them. If you leave them on the floor, they will not be washed and you will have to wash them yourself at the weekend.* Of course, you must then follow through. Once you have done this a couple of times, the child will get the message that actions, and inactions, have consequences. The child can choose, and the consequences follow. If they don't do their

---

23 *Building the Bonds of Attachment: Awakening Love in Deeply Troubled Children*, Dan Hughes.

chores, they don't get to watch TV. You don't have to repeat yourself a hundred times, which reduces your frustration.

It is very easy to become a total hard-ass parent using therapeutic parenting. To combat this, you need to make even more of an effort to praise your child at every available opportunity, just as you would a very young child. Many children with traumatic histories may not have had that developmental period of loving encouragement during their infancy and toddlerhood. Think of it as putting a dollar in the bank towards their self-esteem and ability to self-regulate.

As previously mentioned, children who have suffered trauma will have difficulty self-regulating. They may live in a world dominated by fearful emotions, with their heart racing, spending a lot of energy scanning for threats. They are in a state of constant alertness, and thus cannot access the higher levels of brain functioning – the rational thinking part of the brain. This means they cannot easily talk themselves down. They are more likely to react to what others would consider a trivial matter, blowing it all out of proportion, or to see slights where there are none. Indeed, they may invent a reality that accords to their worldview: that no one can really be trusted except themselves.

When you know this as a parent, putting your child in a situation where they have lots of freedom and few boundaries does not seem like a good idea. It simply sets them up to fail and causes additional stress, which then merely confirms what the child already believes: adults are unreliable.

Therapeutic parenting works because you supply the boundaries, relieving the child of a little bit of stress and creating a bit of a stress-buffer. Over time, this buffer can grow and you can loosen the boundaries a fraction at a time. By saving them from failure, you prevent any damage to their self-esteem. You also save your own mental energy and familial relationships. A win-win situation, if ever there was one.

So what sort of boundaries should you set? Obviously, it depends on the child. Typical flash points might be a birthday party, a family gathering, playing with friends, and partaking in sports teams or after-school activities. Your presence ensures some level of comfort and regulation, and you can, and *must*, interact to keep your child close enough and make decisions for them to ensure their regulation.

Therapeutic parenting may appear over-the-top to your family and friends and, of course, it would be for a non-traumatised child. Some people you can educate, and some people you cannot. Those who you *can* educate can often provide opportunities for positive, non-judgemental relational interactions with the child as they develop; for example, a firm but fair aunt and uncle who make a special effort with the child.

Therapeutic parenting keeps a dysregulated child safe and cuts out a lot of the emotion for parents seeking to give a child direction and expecting them to comply. This, in turn, reduces stress in the household for everyone and facilitates relationship-building. Over time and with other therapeutic interventions, the boundaries can be slowly moved, relaxed or tightened as the child goes through the inevitable ups and downs of their development.

For one of our families, therapeutic parenting was the only thing that changed behaviours in a very angry, controlling child.

Therapeutic parenting has been used successfully with three of our six adopted children.

Positive Relational
Interactions

As you come out of the haze of the early days of adoption, and as your attachment with your child reaches a place that supports widening their circle (and building *your* village), understand the need for and power of relational health for your child.

Positively reinforcing self-esteem is vital for growing confidence and creating a deep-seated sense of safety in your child. Of course, parents provide for the day-to-day needs of the family, but remember to play ball or skip with your child, do craft activities, go on a bike ride, or whatever.

It's also important to create as many opportunities as possible for your child to interact positively with other suitably mature people. This could be a sports coach, a friendly neighbour who walks his dog with your child, or a special aunt or uncle who makes a fuss of them. These interactions do not need to be lengthy – a teacher from a previous grade that says hi and takes an interest in a 30-second conversation may be all that it takes for that day.

Having other people around who take a positive interest in your child reinforces their sense of security and gives you a bit of respite. Note I am not talking about paid help, like counsellors or tutors.

From time to time, usually at the start of a school year, sit back and consider your child's circle beyond your immediate family. If there are not enough people providing positive interactions, think of ways to change this. Many family and friends would love to help, but they often aren't sure exactly what you need, especially if you've been cautious around early attachment.

Each of our families works hard to ensure we have a close-knit and reliable circle of family and friends around our children.

Kinesiology

Through lots of trial and error, coupled with my own research and training, I determined that many of my child's unusual physical behaviours were linked to sensory issues. I also believe she had blocked body reflexes as a result of genetically-linked trauma she inherited from her birth mother, that could have been formed in utero, during delivery or in early infancy.

My research on how to work on these issues led me to kinesiology, which is the study of human movement and how it is linked to the brain; how the brain is wired; and how movement can aid in brain development.

When I took my girl to her first session, she was about six years old and I happened to have my infant biological child with me at the appointment. I must admit, I started off skeptical, but it was a trusted adoptive mother friend who had suggested it, so I wanted to give it a go.

The therapist performed a few basic muscle tests on my girl. These were non-intrusive, and just involved touching points on her arms and ankles. I was blown away as she explained that every infant reflex in her body was totally blocked. The belief is that there is a domino-effect in our bodies in these situations, and until we unblock those early conception reflexes (which could have been blocked due to trauma in the birth mother, bad health, poor diet, circumstances surrounding conception, etc.), other reflexes will remain blocked, often into adulthood. This is why impulse control, self-regulation, stress and anxiety are often difficult to manage.

She pointed out where the differences were in my baby, who was happily playing beside us. Within minutes, she showed me how all her reflexes were unblocked and developing normally for a child who had not experienced trauma.

My girl has continued to see the "relaxing brain lady" with varying regularity. If all is well, she'll see her annually. If she's struggling, we'll see her quarterly.

The therapist helps to tease out a specific anxiety (the first one we worked on was a blocked fear reflex that something was going to happen to me, her mum). She then works on specific exercises to deal with these (touching pressure points, right and left brain crossing, doodling, breathing, etc.). My girl loves it, and even if it's only a maintenance therapy, I would definitely recommend having a go.

I even went for my own "reflex balance" and found out a few interesting things about myself.

◆ ◆ ◆

Kinesiology was highly beneficial for my son. The effects were immediate and tangible, which was such a relief after so many therapies had taken so long to have any effect.

Educational kinesiology in particular was a lifesaver: my son was at an age where his peers were reading, but he was not ready. His basic reflexes were blocked, so teaching him to read was like pouring water into a bucket with holes. One session demonstrated that he couldn't yet track with his eyes. The kinesiologist helped him through some exercises, and then set some exercises for us to do at home. Within three days of performing these exercises, he could track with his eyes. Having something so simple, yet so important become easy for a struggling child is uplifting. I highly recommend it.

Kinesiology is a therapy that has been used successfully with two of our six adopted children.

Equine Therapy

Equine therapy – or more simply, horse riding – has been the only activity that has changed my child's body, persona and mind. As she mounts that horse, her rigid and awkward body relaxes into a soft and natural state. She is graceful, confident and at ease during every minute of her time with the horses. She adores going.

As she is a child who has never attached herself to anything beyond people – she cares little for material things, her education, or her activities – this is emotional for me.

It's wonderful when, after so much searching, you find the "thing" that hits the button of a child. It's especially wonderful when the child typically shows little interest in most things, in which case it can be life-changing.

For the time being, it's working. It calms her, it excites her and it gives her something each week to look forward to. Her uncles (my adored little brothers) have promised to buy her a horse when she thinks she's old enough to care for one independently.

❖ ❖ ❖

When my son is around horses, his body melts. He has always found it very difficult to cuddle and relax against us when we show him affection. The difference when he is with horses is incredible. Horses adore him. They nuzzle into him and trust him completely. When he sits on a horse, his first instinct is to lie on them and wrap his arms around their necks. His body moulds to theirs, and his usually stiff muscles relax. Though he is yet to master a rider's posture, the joy and relaxation that the interaction gives him makes the effort worthwhile.

Equine therapy has been used successfully with two of our six adopted children.

Imaginary Play Therapy

When I see my four children playing together with nothing but their imaginations, I see their innocence. I see their worries disappear, and I see the minds of the babies and toddlers they once were return for a moment. I savour these moments of their childhoods, as our adopted kids had little opportunity for imaginary play in their early years. Even as my children approach secondary school, they enjoy imaginary play just as much as their toddler sister, because they missed out when they were toddlers themselves.

One of our favourite things to do as a family is to travel to wild and wacky places around the world – often so wild that Wi-Fi and TV are non-existent. All the kids have to amuse themselves is each other, and I often tell them that this is why we chose to have a large family and remind them how lucky they are to have each other as siblings. While they are at each other's throats a huge percentage of the time, when we remove the grind of daily life and go off the beaten track for a bit of forced bonding, they often really do bond and unite.

It melts my heart when they play "mums and dads on holiday". They board fictitious taxis and planes, cook imaginary food, hug and cradle each other whilst pretending to feed each other bottles and wrap one another in blankets. They ring fake telephones, use countless imaginary names and places, and each take up different roles in the pecking order of their little pretend sibling life. They talk about their future imaginary house in the mountains with water slides in the garden, a helicopter on the drive, pet hamsters in their bedrooms, and spy cameras so they can see in the dark.

In these moments, I can see a weight being lifted off those precious little shoulders that normally carry so much of a burden to fit in. If I could bottle up this feeling for them and uncork it every time I see anxiety kicking in, I would. Instead, I can only try to provide as many opportunities as possible for them to explore, and protect their childhoods for as long as possible.

◆   ◆   ◆

We have a rule in our house that during the week, there is no access to any screens. This means that it's special for us to watch a movie together on the weekend. We all snuggle together under blankets on the couch, and learn valuable negotiating skills when deciding on the movie.

The best thing about this rule, though, is what happens when the children only have each other and some simple toys to amuse them. Their imaginations come to life. Wooden blocks and twigs become villages and mansions and water parks. The children run outside and become superheroes or wild animals. I see them moving their bodies, exercising their brains and feeling happy and relaxed. Of course, there are many momentary disagreements and even full-blown fights, but I am grateful that they have these opportunities to learn how to work with others, how to sort out their disagreements and continue with their game. It is interesting to watch the roles they play as the sibling pecking order is revealed. It also provides opportunities to discuss standing up for oneself, or being more considerate of others if the same pattern of behaviour is displayed often. It is noisier and messier than allowing the children to sit in front of a TV or iPad, but it is definitely worth the hassle. The content, exhausted bodies that fall into bed at night are a great reward.

Play therapy is something we should all try...

Exercise Therapy

Like all parents, we encourage our kids to play outside, and ferry them around to sports to keep them active. We have some kids who are pretty lazy, some who never stop, and some who are in between. Whatever the child's natural energy level, though, we see a tangible difference when they do a proper bout of exercise that raises their heart rate.

It feels slightly prison-ish to order them to get on the treadmill and finish a certain number of minutes of exercise. We have done this with older kids (those who are over ten), but would struggle to do so with the younger ones. With them, we play games that keep them running or skipping.

While exercise therapy is a relatively new parenting addition for us, the results are gratifyingly instant (unlike most things in the adoptive parenting world, where change is glacial). Get your child exercising and you will notice a difference in their mood right away!

If they are anything like ours, they will complain about doing it, stop and start a lot, step off the treadmill as soon as you turn your back, need lots of pep talking as they do it and, once finished, deny that it has had any impact. But it makes an obvious difference. I also like the secondary benefit of the kids seeing that regular effort leads to improvement in their overall fitness and boosts their ability to push through (well, hopefully, at least).

So what's the theory behind this? It's fascinating, and came from a book my husband was reading called *Spark*.[24] Not only does cardio cause a release of dopamine (the reward chemical in the brain), it also balances other neurochemicals in the brain. Cardio is linked with better mental health, lower risk of heart disease and diabetes, helps balance hormones, and improves school test scores – all backed up by science.

◆　◆　◆

Sometimes, when our son is feeling angsty and disorganised, getting him to exercise (even just for five minutes) can make a huge difference. If we are somewhere that he cannot run around freely, getting him to jump up and down on the spot and push hard against me allows him to use his muscles and feel his body, which in turn helps to reorganise his brain and calm him down. Often at restaurants, my husband or I will take him outside for a quick running and jumping session for immediate calming. It works a treat.

◆　◆　◆

Here are some tips for using exercise as therapy:

◊　Ensure your child is getting the right amount of exercise, at the right intensity, to raise their heart rate and properly make a difference. A game of basketball will do the trick, but a slower-moving game like cricket won't.

◊　Buy them some nice running shoes to encourage them, or bribe them with the promise of new shoes after a number of consistent sessions.

◊　Expect the kids to argue and resist you. I will remove privileges if they don't do their session, and they now understand that.

◊　Try to ensure you use this therapy on days where they are likely to be sedentary, eg. before a long journey

---

24 *Spark: The Revolutionary New Science of Exercise and the Brain*, John J. Ratey

◈ Do it with them. I hate seeing therapists and coming away with a laundry list of more jobs for me. Try to incorporate both your and your child's exercise routines into the same session – you stay sane and your mood is moderated, too.

◈ Be creative if you can't go to a gym or run outside. There are loads of short, intense workouts online.

Exercise therapy has been used successfully (kind of – it's really still a work in progress) with three of our six adopted children.

Occupational Therapy

E ach of us has used occupational therapy at different stages and for different issues with our children, with varying degrees of success.

The development of skills that we take for granted (eg. pincer grip, chewing food, crawling) can be greatly delayed, or even completely missed, in a child who has been in an institution for periods as short as a few months. An occupational therapist (OT) can help with specific exercises and activities that target those particular skills and help them to develop. Skipping milestones (like crawling) can impact on the child's future development and higher learning, so an OT can assist in ways that can have a bearing on all areas of the child's development.

Sensory issues are a significant problem for children who have been in an institution, particularly during infancy. If the child has been mainly left in a cot, the only senses fully activated are hearing and smell, which can become highly over-sensitive, while the other senses are underdeveloped. The OT will be able to prescribe activities to deal with whatever sensory issues your child might have.

We've always had the greatest success when we've paired occupational therapy with the NMT mapping of our child's brain.

This meant that the OT prescribed could be very targeted at helping the brain move past its trauma, at going back and filling in important parts of a child's developmental sequencing.

We could see one of our daughters was struggling in so many ways with her sense of self, and her learning. What we did not realise was how much of this was caused by the stages of brain development that she seems to have skipped. As we reviewed the results from the brain mapping, things that had annoyed us for years all of a sudden made sense: her lack of balance and clumsiness; her regular travel sickness and propensity to vomit; how quickly she became tired.

The recommendations we received were very focused on physical activities that worked carefully on her "gaps". She had a swing in her room, she had to roll around so many times a day, she had to sit on a one-legged stool while she watched TV, and we had to use the body brush on her in a particular way. While she moaned about it initially, within just a few days she was craving it and said she felt a bit off without it.

◆   ◆   ◆

Here are some tips for using occupational therapy:

◊   Find an occupational therapist who understands the impact of trauma on the brain, or is at least interested in learning more from you.

◊   Seriously consider pairing it with NMT brain mapping – doing so has allowed us to feel that the effort we're putting in is having a very specific impact.

Occupational therapy has been used successfully (kind of – it's really still a work in progress) with each of our six adopted children.

Pet Therapy

For nine years, we resisted getting pets. We dabbled with a couple of goldfish and guinea pigs, but things didn't work out (mainly for the pets). Since that early foray, the kids intermittently spoke about wanting a dog. We liked the idea in theory; we knew the potential benefits of caring for an animal and receiving its unconditional love. In practice, when we looked at how the kids struggled to keep their rooms and their persons anywhere near clean, to do small jobs around the house, even to finish homework, a pet felt like another "to-do" nag to add to our long list. And personally, I had no interest in picking up dog poo.

Then one of the kids had an extended run of bad times. It was the usual "who am I, where am I, where do I fit in" angst so common of her age group, but amplified in the adopted child. We were struggling to shift our child out of this funk and it was getting more serious – depression, anxiety, and suicidal thoughts.

Desperate to bring some sunshine to her life to supplement the therapists, psychologists, and me asking, "Are you alright, really?" we caved in on the pet issue right before her birthday. We switched from boisterous dog to lazy cat – a ginger male tabby cat was the request. I searched the Internet for a couple of weeks, and one particular sweet little cat kept drawing me back. While we were living in a big city with plenty of animal rescue shelters around, this cat was a couple of hours' drive north. So off we went to pick up our new family member.

We drove this cat home, and he instantly made sense. He bolstered the sense of home, of belonging, of love when you walked in the door. All of us spoke, a bit surprised, about how much we enjoyed having him around, and agreed less than two weeks later to drive north again to pick up his sister.

So now we have two little cats, both of whom didn't get off to a great start in life, but who are enjoying being fed on time, having free rein over the house, being picked up and cuddled whenever the kids are home, and laying in the sun while they are at school.

I've seen the kids grow in their confidence in interacting with them, understanding that the cats gravitate to the person showing them love calmly – and learning that you reap what you sow in a relationship.

I see my girl increasingly calm and centred. The first thing she does when she walks in the door after school is scoop up one of the cats and cuddle them; she is home, and can leave whatever has happened during the day outside.

I see my other children learning to love an animal, to treat animals with respect, and I hope this spills into their lives more broadly. It's funny: the cats teach them exactly the things we've been trying to teach them about love and relationships for years, but they do it so effectively, and with no words.

When I think of pets as therapy, the last person I expected to benefit from it was me, the well-adjusted mother. I, too, look forward to laying down with a kitten on my lap after a busy day; I take great pleasure in stroking them and watching them bliss out at the human contact. I am now officially a crazy cat lady, and I don't know why we didn't become a cat family years ago.

My husband, a dog man from way back, has also been surprised by how much he enjoys them: how much personality they have, how the two cats can be so different to each other, how they truly make good company.

If you're thinking a pet might help your family, don't think twice – just do it. I wish we had done this years ago. A pet is a big commitment, but you've already got children, so I figure you're over that hurdle.

Investigate what kind of pet will suit your family: you want it to fit into the family groove, not create a bunch of tasks that you never had before. If you don't have a big yard, or regularly walk the kids to school or to the shops, don't get a big dog. If your kids will need a lot of feedback from their animal, maybe a cat won't be the best option, as they can be stand-offish at times. If you're worried you don't yet have the capacity to care for a pet, or that your kids aren't in the headspace to do so, consider a low maintenance, hardy pet like a tortoise or a lizard.

And all this from someone who would previously have said I wasn't much into animals.

◆ ◆ ◆

We delayed getting a dog while we were travelling around and moving often, as it wasn't practical. When we finally settled for a few years, we adopted a tiny rescue puppy. He was our baby. The whole family loved and cared for this puppy, with fights often breaking out over whose turn it was to hold him. The children treated him like their baby (and I loved it when they were all in bed and I got him all to myself!).

After a year, we decided he needed a friend, and adopted another rescue puppy. While all of the children love the dogs, none more so than our adopted son. He has a special bond with our second dog. She was at the pound for longer than the first. She suffers from a bit of anxiety and is very nervous with new people. When they are together, they simply connect. Their bodies relax and he whispers calm words in her ear while stroking her gently. Seeing him care for someone in such an empathetic and mature way warms my heart. He understands her anxiety, and he knows how to help her overcome it. They are kindred spirits who share a similar past and find comfort in each other. She provides him things that I never could, and I am so grateful he has these dogs in his life.

◆ ◆ ◆

Pets not only help our children to feel calm and loved, they also teach them about life and death. Our son is responsible for feeding our chickens in the morning. He loves this job and feels responsible for the chickens. Unfortunately, one of our chickens recently died. All of the children were sad, but none more so than him.

We held a little service for the chicken, and he cried uncontrollably. He feels the pain of separation more than the other children. Leaving people behind when we have moved was never that hard for the others, but he has felt it deeply, wailing and crying desperately. Our cat also died a couple of years ago, and he cried for hours.

To experience the pain of grief and to understand that it gets better and you can move on is an invaluable lesson that our children are learning. While I understand that the death of a cat or a chicken would, in no way, prepare you for the loss of a loved one, it does help the children to understand that death is a part of life. It happens and you feel it, and eventually you can move past it and on with your life.

Pet therapy has been universally successful with five of our six adopted children. My apologies to our eldest child, who grew up in a pet-free house.

Meditation as Therapy

Just the word "meditation" puts off a lot of people. They think of it as a skill that takes years to master, and that you need to be an orange-robed vegan hippie. Not so.

Anyone can learn basic, effective meditation in five minutes. We strongly believe that there isn't a person or personality type that isn't helped by a meditation practice. The challenge with wriggly kids – particularly extra-wriggly, short attention-spanned adopted kids – is to pick the moment and the meditation that have the highest chance of impact.

Our advice on how to incorporate meditation into daily life is to use it at bedtime. Instead of screaming at them to hurry up and go to sleep, put on a meditation soundtrack, and they will wiggle and squirm and eventually listen. They calm down, their bodies slow, they listen intently to the meditation and, sure enough, fall asleep. I will sit on their floor and use this time to meditate myself. It doesn't matter that it's a child-focused meditation. What's most important is that I'm sitting and doing it, and it still ticks the boxes for me.

I notice that when we get out of this habit, bedtime gets shouty until I eventually remember to re-incorporate meditation into our routine.

Links to our favourite meditation soundtracks are in the Resources section of our website.[25]

◆   ◆   ◆

Teaching your child how to meditate anywhere, anytime is an absolute gift to them, for life. If they are struggling to concentrate at school, or if they are feeling overwhelmed and don't know what to do, this will help them to self-manage. Of course, the simple method we describe below is also excellent for harried parents and we have a video to teach children to do this on our website.

Firstly, get your child to focus on the breath coming in and going out of the nose. Notice the sensation of breath entering and leaving the body. It is not about having a blank mind, but an awareness of self. Allow thoughts to come and go without judgement. When you notice that your attention has wandered from breathing to what you are having for dinner, simply return your attention to the breath and let go of your dinner thoughts. Try meditating like this for two minutes, and build up over time to ten or 15 minutes. If you do this at bedtime, just like with the guided meditation videos above, you will find your child has a deep, relaxing sleep afterwards.

Another simple meditation method, if your child needs a little more guidance and activity, is to breathe in as you count 1-2-3-4, hold the breath 1-2-3-4, and release the breath 1-2-3-4-5-6. I do this often, and it calms me down immediately.

My children like to combine meditation with the gentle sounds of a singing bowl. They love it when they are lying down and I put the singing bowl on their back. The vibrations resonate through them and calm them immensely.

◆   ◆   ◆

If you have a child with anxiety and low self-esteem, gratitude and loving-kindness practices can help.

When my child was struggling at school for a few months, we'd

---

25 www.lionheartfamilies.com/resources

listen to a three- or five-minute Loving Kindness meditation on the Calm app, and this would help reset her mind as she approached starting her day. Even if we didn't have time for her to listen, I'd give her a short shoulder massage and repeat to her, "May you be happy, may you be healthy, may you live in peace."

Meditation as therapy has been used successfully with three of our six adopted children.

Simple Ideas for Sensory Feedback Therapy and Massage Therapy

My boy needs sensory feedback like he needs to breathe. If he walks down a street, he needs to jump, run and slide his hand along the various fences. If he eats, he munches and crunches and slurps. If he swims, he throws himself around, smashes, crashes, does handstands and holds his breath. He is constantly pushing his body to feel more, to signal to him, "Hey, you are here," and to keep him calm.

There's a suite of therapeutic options for children who need a lot of sensory feedback. See an Occupational Therapist for an hour a week for various exercises and activities that involve pushing, pulling and pressing. The OT will also provide you with guidance on some activities to try at home, like using a soft body brush to brush your child's arms and legs in bed, or a weighted blanket to sleep under. Another activity to try, just as your child is about to go to sleep, is to have them lie on their bed under their covers while you press on their legs, back and arms – it will relax them beautifully.

But sometimes, if it's between OT sessions, or your child has outgrown some of these exercises, or it's the middle of the day and they can't really lie under a weighted blanket, they might be a bit off, and you will see that they need sensory feedback. In these cases, you need to find some simple fixes at home.

One strategy we will use at home for a simple sensory fix is to get my boy baking. I don't mean lovely cakes, where an electric mixer does all the work. I mean scones, where he has to rub butter and flour together for a long time; pizza dough that he has to knead, prove and then punch and knead again, before rolling it out; bread that he has to mix and knead and mould. You can really punch and stretch dough and get your angst out. Dough is particularly good because it is very sensory, having all that flour and water sticking to your hands and having to knead it. I can see him move into the moment and his body calms, quietens. He also gets the positive experience of some parental time, and he laps up the family compliments. And let's not forget, as a boy who loves to eat, he very much appreciates the fruits of his labour.

Another strategy we use is to get my boy into the sea. We are fortunate to live near the ocean, and he loves being in it. If I take him down to the beach, he'll happily roll about in the waves on our neighbour's hand-me-down surfboard for hours. He gets the smell of the salt, the cool of the water, the pressure of the waves, the expended energy from paddling and standing up. It works even better for him if the weather is cooler and he needs to wear a wetsuit – the compression of the garment only adds to the feedback his body so craves.

Of course, often they'll be craving sensory feedback at school, when they can't just bake a loaf of bread or go surfing. We gave some tips for kids who crave movement in an earlier section. You can always send them to school with a small, squishy OT toy that they can quietly play with. Of course, their teacher needs to be on board with this method. An on-side teacher will think of other ways to work with a wriggly kid as well: one of the children's teachers lets him lay outside to do quiet work, as long as he doesn't disturb others.

If you pack lunches, try to pack sensory-challenged kids a "sensory lunchbox": think of satisfying their need for sensory feedback across as many senses and sensations as possible. We've provided some ideas below. Try and cover a few senses every day; this becomes second nature after a while.

If your child gets a meal at school, encourage them to choose foods that give them some different types of feedback.

Ideas for a Sensory Lunchbox

COLD	JUICY
Frozen grapes	Orange quarters
Frozen fruitbox	Watermelon
CRUNCHY	SPICY
Apples	Salami on sandwiches
Carrots	
Cucumber	WARM
	Soup in a thermos
SQUISHY	
Yoghurt	SALTY
	Popcorn
CHEWY	Pretzels
Dried fruit (really works the jaw!)	Olives
Apricots, sultanas, mango	

We suggested massage therapy back in the "Sleepless Early Days" chapter to try and calm discombobulated children down and improve sleep. Massage therapy is also a great tool for bonding, and for kids with sensory issues. Often when I walk past one of the kids, I'll give them a micro shoulder rub, a head rub, or a foot rub, just for a very short moment. It makes them feel nice and they associate that with me. They feel calmer. They learn that a short massage can calm them down, and are gaining the tools to ultimately self-soothe.

One day, when we were on holidays in Asia (where massage is cheap and available everywhere), all of us filed into a shop and had a massage. We ambled out to put our shoes back on when the time was up, bleary-eyed and chilled – all except our boy who never stops moving. He had fallen asleep on the massage chair, and the therapist couldn't wake him. We sat next to him for ages while he slept like he'd never slept before. That was the moment we saw how massage could calm a kid like him, with sensory issues. Now, whenever we have the opportunity or when he seems out of kilter, we'll take him for a massage and marvel at how relaxed and still he becomes!

◆ ◆ ◆

When we brought our child home, his sensory issues were quite severe. If I applied cream to his skin, he would scream, "Ouch!" The sensation of the cold, wet cream was foreign and interpreted by his brain as pain. Massaging him was out of the question.

After a year or so of intensive OT, he was able to accept massage. Now it's his favourite thing in the world. When we need him to sit quietly (in a restaurant, theatre, etc.), all I have to do is massage him – his hands, head, back, whatever is easily accessible. He becomes jelly in my hands. At night, before bed, he asks me to massage his hands, feet and head. The relaxation is instant and significant. Massage has replaced my irritated pleas for him to sit still and be quiet. It calms both of us and allows us to enjoy the time together, instead of it becoming a struggle.

Sensory therapy has been used successfully with three of our six adopted children.

The Mind-Altering Properties of Chewing Gum

I have always found people chomping away on chewing gum a bit gross. Irreverent, even. And the ads for chewing gum on TV are about as annoying as ads can get.

Many parents ban chewing gum as inappropriate, potentially dangerous, or fairly likely to end up in hair or the carpet. In fact, as a child, my husband once wrapped chewing gum around and around and around his neck. It hardened; then he was in trouble. And he's a sensible one.

I have totally changed my negative views after seeing the impact that chewing gum has on my kids.

Chewing gum is a non-intrusive way to get some sensory feedback, to exercise some muscles while sitting still. It brings focus to the mind. It has an immediate calming effect on some children. Teachers would be well served to tap into the mind-calming influence that chewing gum provides, though I know modern liability concerns would likely make this challenging.

We buy Extra by the bulk packet. After becoming convinced of its usefulness, we happily dispense it to all of our kids when they ask for it, or when we see they need it. Chewing gum as we start homework provides some focus for the mind. Chewing gum as we drive down the coast reduces both carsickness and territorial disputes between siblings. Even I like it if I'm feeling a bit stressed, as I am a jaw-clencher from way back, and chewing gum provides great relief.

I urge you to reconsider if chewing gum is a banned substance for your children.

I was not paid by any chewing gum companies for this recommendation, though am happy to take payment for this endorsement in boxes of chewing gum...

Chewing gum therapy has been used successfully with three of our six adopted children.

Creating Traditions

Traditions link us to our past, our childhood, or even our heritage. You may cook the food that was eaten and remembered from your ancestry, repeat little rituals with your own children that your grandparents did with you, or retell a story that was special to you at some point in your past.

I'm yet to discover why we have a particular Christmas Eve tradition that dates back generations. For as long as I can remember, our family has cooked as many whole roast ducks as our oven could handle, chopped up spring onions and cucumbers, and served the duck with an abundance of wraps and prawn crackers on a coffee table, while we sit on the floor. We don't have any Chinese heritage of which I am aware, but this funny tradition has stuck and is now something my children look forward to in the lead-up to Christmas.

Traditions and rituals often tell a story about a family. On a macro level, they teach your children about their history or their parents' history; but on a more micro level, they play a vital role in shaping the identity of a child as they grow.

Research has found that children who have deep-rooted traditions grow up with a more confident sense of self. Creating traditions can provide a source of constancy in life for an adopted child. Traditions can teach and reinforce values, and create a sense of belonging for your adopted child.

Many of us who have adopted missed months or years of our child's life. We've created this instant family, where it is our responsibility to bond strangers as brothers and sisters. We have found that our kids, having missed so much in the way of normal family life in their early years, hold on hard to the traditions we create for them. We work hard to create them as well, to try to fill their childhood with new, happier memories.

When creating a tradition, think about why you want to do this and what you hope the children will get out of it, now and in years to come. Once you know, move on to personalising it for your family. Some traditions are seasonal or time-bound. What might work for younger kids might be less relevant for older kids (although my brothers, now in their thirties, still like a Santa sack at the end of their bed when they stay at Mum's on Christmas Eve).

While the bigger traditions are wonderful, it's important to create daily and weekly traditions, too. These can be simple things, like dinners together, the routine around bedtimes, and so on.

We've detailed a few of our family favourites below to give you some ideas on how to get started.

◆　◆　◆

Our families are each quite different in our approaches to birthdays.

For two of our families, birthdays are celebrated with presents and a party. One of our kids will start to be a little off a week or two before his birthday. We know to recognise this now, and speak with him about how he is feeling. We've been surprised, though, that the other kids haven't been more sad in the lead-up to their birthdays.

For one of our families, birthdays bring a sense of sadness that we find hard to shift as adults. We think about birth family and what they have suffered. For some of the kids, we don't know their birthday or the circumstances of their birth; because of this, our birthday celebrations tend to be more about being another year older, and not talking about the day they were born.

While we get melancholy around birthdays, we haven't seen the kids pick up the same feelings. They are happy to celebrate at a superficial level, not dwelling on the "birth" part of birthday.

We feel that each child's birthday is simply a celebration of their life: the fact that they exist, they are another year older and wiser, and we get to celebrate it together. These are all things to be grateful for.

◆ ◆ ◆

Family day is another occasion some of us celebrate. On family day, we remember the day a child was adopted into our family. It's reasonably low key – just a sponge cake and a chat about our memories.

Another one of our families calls it adoption day – the day our son officially became ours. He loves it: he gets special treatment all day, a cake and a fuss. His siblings are envious (the best bit of the day), and it's just another excuse for our family to celebrate. We try to breed gratitude in our family, finding things to be grateful for every day. And our son's adoption is a huge thing for our family to be grateful for.

We like using the terms "family day" or "adoption day". We don't like the very widely used "Gotcha Day" (sorry!). We find the language overly-focused on the parents' excitement and the end of their usually long and arduous journey. We totally understand a desire to celebrate the end of that; however, we find it a little insensitive to the child and their birth family, and the word makes me think of taking something from someone. It's a special day to mark, but does it need to be "Gotcha"?

◆ ◆ ◆

We love Easter and Christmas, and have each created some traditions that are now non-negotiable. For example, one of us always hosts a great big Easter lunch with a rowdy egg hunt afterwards.

At Christmas, one of us has Christmas dinner on Christmas Eve, and everyone receives a gift of new pyjamas and a book. The next day is then freed up as we can eat leftovers instead of cooking, leaving all the time in the world to enjoy new presents!

Another one of us has a tradition of naughty Santa. He always wreaks havoc on their house somehow – he might pull all the boxes out of the pantry onto the floor and throw cereal around; he might throw talcum powder all over the windows!

Close to Christmas each year, we'll take the family camping at the same campground. We all enjoy the freedom of being outside – collecting firewood, peeing in the desert, the excitement of sleeping in a tent. The best part is toasting marshmallows over a fire – we'll make any excuse to toast marshmallows, even when it's not cold.

◆   ◆   ◆

Picnics have featured in our family tradition arsenal in a few ways. One of our families, lazy at the end of a week, once threw a checked blanket on top of the playroom rug and had Japanese takeaway on the floor. This floor picnic of gyozas and teriyaki chicken became our Friday night ritual for the couple of years we lived in that particular house.

It can be surprising to find yourself repeating childhood traditions. To find the perfect picnic spot, we used to drive around looking for a place my aunty deemed 10/10. Under no circumstances would we stop for a 9/10! As we drove around, my aunty would shout out the score, but no one understood the criteria; all she ever said was, "It's not a bonny view." We follow the same principle now when searching for a picnic spot.

Another picnic tradition that has been carried through to the next generation is carrier bag picnics. You choose your food from the cupboards, anything you want; and put it into a plastic bag. My mother does this each time she stays: the kids and mum hike around, each carrying their own plastic bag, and then they sit on the ground and eat their picnic. It's very low key, super easy and, just like I did, the kids love it. They ask to do it all the time.

◆   ◆   ◆

Of course, food features strongly in our family traditions. We like it comforting, we like it easy, and we like it in quantities enough to feed a small army.

Both Selina and Jodie use a couple of Tammie's very simple recipes when we're feeding a tribe (Tammie is an awesome cook – she would say these aren't her best recipes, but our kids adore them!). One is Tammie's Chicken Legs (she doesn't have legs like a chicken, for the record), and the other is Tammie's Tuna Pasta. The latter is a recipe we teach our kids to cook as they hit high school. Both recipes are on our website.[26]

For Selina, Aunty Evy's Rice Pudding has been a staple throughout her life, and now every month, she and the kids will cook up a cauldron of it and freeze it. The kids will take a little pot out every few days and microwave it when they need sweet comfort. Aunty Evy was stoked that we asked for her recipe to share here.

Aunty Evy's Rice Pudding: Foolproof Recipe

The trick is a thick-bottomed pot and PATIENCE!

Ingredients:

8 heaped tablespoons of pudding rice (risotto rice is also fine)
One pint of full-fat milk (Jersey cream milk is even better)
One large can of evaporated milk
4-6 tablespoons of sugar

Put the ingredients into a pot and bring to a soft boil. Keep stirring whilst simmering for 10 to 15 minutes. Take off the heat.

This part is important: put the lid on and leave it for 20 to 30 minutes.

Variation: once the cooking is done, pour into a buttered ovenproof dish and put a few knobs of butter on the top. Bake at 180 degrees (Celsius) for about 30 minutes. This will caramelise the top.

Enjoy!

Aunty Evy

---

26 www.lionheartfamilies.com/resources

Selina has another tradition she's building around Saturday dinner. She says that as the kids grow and become more independent, the one thing she will always insist on, just like her mother did, is that they are all home and sitting around the table for Saturday dinner. This is a calm and peaceful break in the busy week, and a chance to reconnect.

Jodie had a sweet tradition in the early years of her family – madeleines for breakfast on Saturday morning. In Dubai, you could buy French madeleines from the supermarket that were simply lovely. They would dip them in coffee, the kids in hot milk. They did this for two years before moving home. She made some madeleines recently and the wistful nostalgia that came over the face of one of the kids was beautiful. If you ever wonder whether they notice these little traditions, don't – they are most definitely having an impact.

Jodie's family has another tradition that is an evolution of their old floor picnics: Friday night fish and chips. This is the night where they make oven fish and chips. No vegetables, no bits the kids hate. They don't have to sit at the table, and they can watch TV as they eat. They love it.

One of Tammie's family's favourite food traditions is whenever they are travelling, if their hotel has congee for breakfast, she and her boy will race each other downstairs for breakfast so they can both eat it. Her boy loves that his mother likes Cambodian food.

Actually, most of Tammie's family traditions revolve around food! Every night at dinner, each member of the family has a turn telling everyone their "highs and lows" – the best part and the worst part of the day. They are allowed one low, but as many highs as they like – with six people in the family, there needs to be some limitations, or dinner would take all night! This rule also encourages the family to share their day and focus on things they are grateful for. The lows are, of course, important to talk about, and often having to share a low encourages a child to disclose things that might otherwise have gone unmentioned.

◆ ◆ ◆

Given that we were Australians and Brits living in Dubai, and that we have kids from West Africa and Asia, it's perhaps understandable that we travel a fair bit.

With four kids each, the cost can be prohibitive, but we all agree that the life experiences of travel are so immense that we'd rather spend our money on this than, say, a fancy car.

Of course, travel broadens the worldviews of the kids, but there are a couple of other reasons we make it a priority. One is that when we travel, we are all stuck with each other in close proximity, without any of us having the usual jobs and distractions. The best memories of our decade of parenting have been made on holidays. The other is that travel is often to see someone – a beloved friend or close relative. This helps with the crucial relational health of adopted children that we referenced earlier.

It might only be for a weekend away, but in that weekend we see and hear each other properly.

If you subscribe to our Instagram (@lionheartfamilies) or Facebook feeds (www.facebook.com/lionheartfamilies), you can follow along on some of our adventures.

Parental Self-Care

———◇———

"I have come to believe that caring for myself is not self-indulgent. Caring for myself is an act of survival."
Audre Lorde

———◇———

Section Contents

A Really Bad Day

To set the scene for why parental self-care is a vital, yet often overlooked part of adoptive parenting, let us share a story.

I had a newborn baby and a newly adopted child who had been home for only a few weeks. At that point, I was under the illusion that I could still do everything I had done with one child. One day, I almost broke from my efforts.

On paper, it doesn't sound so bad: we needed to do a grocery shop and then go to the doctor's office for vaccinations for both new children. The grocery shop was far more difficult to manage, but I was organised with snacks in my bag and a measured, patient voice for the two bigger kids. The newborn was asleep. I was slaying this three-child parenting.

Next, we were off to the doctor's surgery. He and I agreed we should give the older child the vaccinations first, so she didn't get upset after watching the baby get his. I was a pro at this, and the doctor and I were a well-oiled machine. I sat my girl on my lap as the doctor prepared the little tray with his back to us, before swiftly turning and plunging it into her little arm. But my eldest was watching. This was not *her* first rodeo, and she knew what was happening. Her eyes widened and she jumped into protector mode. Before the doctor or I could take in what was happening, she had lunged at the syringe and ripped it out of her sister's arm. Both of the girls screamed, the vaccinated one and the almost-vaccinated one. The baby woke up and started screaming. Blood spurted everywhere. My eldest was screaming at the top of her lungs, with anger I'd never seen from her at that point, *"Do NOT hurt my sister!"* The doctor and I wearily agreed to leave it to another day. I hadn't thought for a second that I should have explained to our biggest girl what was happening and why.

I hauled the three kids back out to the car. I strapped in the baby and got the eldest to wait while I crawled over to the back of the car with her newly adopted sister. I had, by this time, learned that she couldn't sit next to the baby, as she would pick up things (often the stainless steel water bottles we had in the car) and pelt them at the newborn baby's head. I then strapped my eldest in and we drove home, still a symphony of screams and crying.

My new girl's mood had snapped and shifted dramatically. It seemed, prompted by her big sister's reaction, that at some level she felt I'd broken her trust and hurt her.

I was happy to get home, knowing we didn't have to leave the house again that day. I let the girls play as the baby slept in the capsule next to me and I quickly made lasagna. My friends laughed at me for the time I gave the kids dinner and put them to bed. I knew today they were going really, really early; bowls of lasagna were on the table by 3pm. Bedtime was within reach. My new girl sat at the table, picked up her bowl, and launched it at the baby. He whimpered as (thankfully warm, not steaming hot) lasagna covered him.

She was strapped into a very stable wooden high chair (actually, I will give it a shout out: the Tripp Trapp Stokke chair. They saved me in the early days), and rocked and writhed back and forth around the kitchen. Then she started building up spit in her mouth and forcing snot to run from her nose. I could do little else but wipe béchamel sauce off my baby. I was sad and angry at the same time. What kind of danger was I putting this baby in? What if the food had been straight out of the oven? What if it had landed in his eyes?

Eventually I had things under control enough to put the girls in the bath while I sat beside the bath feeding the baby. The same girl who had protected her little sister from the needle now saw there was no such thing as *quid pro quo*. Her little sister started grabbing her by the hair and pushing her head under the bath water. I'd jump up and stop it; then she'd attempt to drown her big sister again as soon as I sat back down. I'd stop it and sit down. She'd try to drown her again. This went on until I'd had enough. I got them out the bath, trying to carry these two toddlers and a baby at the same time. They all needed drying, they all needed cream, and then they all needed their pajamas on.

By that point, I didn't know how I was going to parent these kids without killing one of them. Or, more to the point, without one of them killing another. Somehow, I hauled them downstairs into the TV room, sat them inside and locked the door. I was attempting nothing more until my husband got home. I didn't care if we sat there all night; I could physically do no more.

My angry child started her rampage. She grabbed the cushions off the sofas and threw them onto the floor. She pulled over CD cabinets and emptied them out, CD by CD. All the while, her big sister sat happily watching Barney, her head off somewhere else (if only!), while I sat and rocked myself and fed the baby.

Every few minutes, I'd put the baby down and go and sit with my angry child and hug her. I knew I had to give her the attention she craved. I looked her in the eyes and said, "Mummy doesn't like it when you throw things on the floor. Mummy knows you are sad." She'd seem to calm a little, and would come and sit on the sofa with me. I'd start to relax again. Before long, the baby would need something. As soon as I picked him up, she'd look me in the eyes and start again. Stick out her arm and swipe everything off the coffee table in one fell swoop. The CDs all over the floor again, the cushions everywhere.

She turned her attention to aggravating her sister. She'd run up and pinch her. Grab the remote and turn Barney off. As I responded with requests to turn the TV back on, she'd keep escalating her behaviour.

Funnily enough, her big sister never hated her. She'd had all the attention from her parents, and then suddenly, within short order, had a wild little sister and a baby brother. She cared little that her sister seemingly wanted to kill her. They would dance around the lounge room together, the little one chanting, "Aunty... aunty... aunty," and the big one chanting, "Jojo coming... Jojo coming."

After a while, I stood up to turn the TV off, and my angry girl saw the moment was right to get at the baby. She started yanking hard at my arm, trying to get me to drop him. I shouted at her to stop and she dropped to the floor, writhing around and squealing.

She had pushed me to my limit within just a few weeks of being home. I was so disappointed with myself. I was so angry with her. I looked at her and let myself imagine how satisfying it would be to lunge at her. I don't physically discipline the kids at all, and yet I could feel how out of control I was getting.

I called my husband at work, pulled him out of a meeting and, for the first time ever, told him he needed to come home *now*. This day is definitely in the running for my worst adoptive parenting day ever.

Regular Self-Care

Your child *will* drive you mad. Understanding trauma helps to comprehend the reasons behind some of the behaviour; but it will still not prevent you from sometimes being annoyed, exasperated and angry as you explain *for the thousandth time* why your child cannot do something, and they know this but do it anyway. Again! *How many times...* Managing your own stress levels is crucial, as stress has been shown to be a causative factor of many serious diseases and reduces the body's immune system.

Many adoptive parents feel overwhelmed by their issues and think self-care is just around the corner. When we fix this, when we have done that, then I will do something for me.

Managing your own stress is essential to avoiding burnout – a.k.a. giving up. It is no wonder that some foster placements and adoptions with very caring people end up failing. Parenting children with trauma can be extremely difficult. We cover these very real feelings in the "I Give Up" chapter.

It is crucial to make self-care part of your daily routine. We know that it sounds fanciful when you've got an argumentative child, a child who doesn't sleep, calls from the school with concerns, and a list of appointments as long as your arm. But taking ten minutes here and there just for you will provide some relief and enable you to better deal with your challenges. Think of it in that way, rather than as just being another job.

What should you do to reduce stress? Some of the things we suggest for your child in the Therapy Toolbox section will work for you, too. Three of our simplest and best strategies are below.

◊ Breathing is a simple and easy strategy. It sounds too simple to be true, in fact, but it is effective. Breathing in and then slowly and purposefully breathing out allows the parasympathetic nervous system to slow the heart rate, reduce blood pressure and restore balance to the mind and body. Thinking about being calm actually *makes* you calm and reduces your heart rate.

◊ Meditation is another simple strategy that pays dividends. We covered it in the Therapy Toolbox section, and everything we said there applies to you as the parent. Incorporating meditation at bedtime is great for everyone. Often, you might need it as you start the day as well. There are some great apps you can use that are free or subscription-based, and that offer various lengths of guided meditation. I use the Calm app, and do the daily meditation most days as I commute to work.

◊ Cardio activity is another excellent strategy. You need to get your heart rate up to really benefit.[27] Sustain this for 15 minutes if you can. It does not matter what the exercise is, as long as you enjoy it. A treadmill is a good option as it is accessible and often has a heart rate monitor. You could also try skipping (very cheap and highly effective, but also a great way to see how unfit you have become!), boxing with a punching bag, swimming, cycling, rowing, etc. Note that while gentler exercise can have other benefits, yoga or walking will not deliver the benefits of a proper cardio session. Neither will lifting weights.

◆　◆　◆

---

27 To calculate what this rate is for you, subtract your age from 220 to find your maximum heart rate, and then calculate 80% of that number. That's how many beats per minute (bpm) you should aim to reach. So, if you are 40 years old, your maximum heart rate is 220 − 40 = 180 bpm; and 80% of that is 144 bpm. See *Spark* by John Ratey, as previously referenced in the Exercise Therapy section.

Here are some ideas on incorporating self-care into your day:

◊ Try and have some respite from care duties, if you can. This is not always possible, and it is never easy. Friends and relatives do not generally have the understanding or capacity to help with this. If there are two parents, try and tag team so one gets a rest while the other takes the child to the park or the movies. Do *not* wait until you are knackered to start thinking about self-care. Your energy depletion is definitely coming, so start getting into good habits now.

◊ Seek some acceptance and understanding from one or two trusted friends or family members. Find a sister, brother, or mother who you can chat with honestly, who won't freak out about what you need to say. An in-the-know family member might be able to watch the kids for an hour so you can go running, have a massage, drink coffee, sip margaritas – whatever it is that restores you. To help your family and friends understand your challenges, we've put together a free two-pager called "What to Expect When Someone You Love is Adopting", which is available through our website.[28]

◊ In general, give yourself enough downtime. Do fewer scheduled activities and classes. When we first started, we probably did too many baby splash and baby dance classes (in fact, Selina and Tammie ran a baby dance class empire in Dubai for a while – true story!). Avoid getting sucked into feeling like you need to do "all of the things". The main thing you should be doing is staying home.

◊ When you're the primary carer, make sure that you get a break. We reckon you need an hour to yourself every day to revive. Have a lie down when the kids are sleeping. Watch some bad TV while they're doing the same. Have a bath. Resist the urge to wash and clean and do whatever – you will soon be running on empty if you're not actively taking some time for yourself.

◊ If you're a single parent, you still need a break. Do you have a friend or relative you can do a "swap" with? It's worth biting off a bucketload of kids for a few hours, in return for a few hours of solitude later.

28 www.lionheartfamilies.com/resources

◈ When you're not the primary carer, make sure you are adept at dealing with the kids. Your partner does it day in, day out; you need to be able to handle them yourself, too. Make sure that you do some special things with the kids and spend plenty of time with them. It can feel hard to know how to start and what to do, especially early on. If you're the parent the child is bonded to, ensure you give the other parent space, too.

◈ Because I'm working full time and travelling a lot, I search out hobbies I can enjoy with the kids. If you aren't into imaginary play, don't spend hours doing this with them. Instead, do the art and craft you love with them. As the kids get older, it is wonderful to develop hobbies in common. You can play guitars and sing together, surf together, do yoga together, or watch football together.

◈ While we were writing this book, we each flew in to Singapore from our respective homes for a long weekend together. These few days together topped up our patience and armed us with a deeper level of understanding of our children. Just when you think you've got it all together, you learn more tips or a different approach, or you find a book you've never read. Regularly spending time with people who really understand you is precious and liberating. Mum weekends away should be a mandatory part of parenting!

◈ Get enough sleep, or try and catch up. If you have a partner, have one of you lie in one day at the weekend, and then the other the next.

◈ Get serious about nutrition – make sure you are eating properly, and not loading up on sugar or junk foods. It is definitely an effort to make nutritious, wholesome foods, but your body and mind will thank you for it. And if you feed it to your children, they will be better off mentally and physically as well. If you have friends and family who want to help, ask them to make you some home-cooked dinners.

When You Are Close to Breaking Point

We've each of us had many days, months and even years where we lived precariously close to breaking point.

When we're in this state, all it takes is a small event to set us off and we blow up like Mount Vesuvius. We have teeny-tiny amounts of patience, and behaviour that normally wouldn't bother us, now *really* bothers us.

Knowing when you're in this place, and finding ways to create some space between yourself and breaking point, is crucial. Some parents use alcohol, contraband bars of chocolate eaten at night or in pantry cupboards when kids aren't looking, hiding under the doona, watching crappy TV. We've been there.

We all have different responses when things get really tough. Self-awareness is key: there's no "right way" to deal with tough times as an adoptive parent, just as there's no "right way" to deal with tough times as a human.

One of us wants distraction when things are tough: to hear stories of normal life, and not get into detail about the hard stuff that's happening until it's no longer a crisis. Her kids have taught her that, contrary to what popular culture would have you believe, talking does *not* make everything better. Talking can make some things feel eternal, ever-present and inescapable. Talking about anything else, watching a distracting movie, or reading an escapist book is far more soothing.

Another of us wants to talk it out. She'll call you and chat about stuff as it is happening (as in, you can occasionally actually hear a child shouting in the background), sharing her frustrations and her ideas on what's going on. She is soothed by discussion, by a sharing of stories, and is comforted to hear that you've had something similar happen and some ideas on what to do.

The third one of us goes into fix-it mode: finding the right therapist, trying this or that, battening down the hatches, gritting her teeth and committing to working on this until it is solved. She knows it might take weeks or months or years, but she's tireless. She often doesn't give lots away or share that she is struggling, bar the offhand comment here or there, until much later.

◆　◆　◆

Here are our go-to approaches for averting a breakdown, learned over a decade of adoptive parenting:

Selina

I always know I'm close to breaking point when I start screaming, "I am not a machine!" at my husband. This is the only phrase that makes sense to me; it's otherwise hard to articulate my feelings.

My personality is hard-wired to survive: I'm a coper (there should be a badge!), and I don't like to show weakness or admit failure. I struggle to admit that I'm finding things tough. So you can be sure that if I do, I'm absolutely at the end of my tether.

I have a strange response when I'm feeling like this, and it's to pile more on to the to-do list. I know it's not rational and I can see it's ridiculous. I've moved house, had endless visitors stay, been studying for my Master's, managed renovations, done volunteer work, worked part-time, been breastfeeding and had a newly adopted child – all in the same month.

When I can hear myself screaming *I am not a machine* when I am, in fact, acting more and more like one in my manic productivity, I have learned that I need to let go a little. I have realised it's OK for the kids to eat pizza for dinner, it's OK for them to have to have no milk on their cereal because you can't be arsed to go to the shop, it's OK to use a sponge to scrub off yoghurt stains on a uniform when washing and drying it seems like a mammoth task that day. It's all OK! They are not going to remember these shortcuts. (Or, so I tell myself. If they do remember, they'll remember it like my brothers and I do when we wind up our Mum: *Remember when you made us jam tarts for dinner? Remember when you glued our Brownie and Scouts badges to our uniform because you couldn't be bothered to sew them?* She steadfastly denies both incidents.)

As I've grown as a parent over the years, I have also realised how important it is for the children to be part of this with me. When I am having a cry or a meltdown, I tell them, "Mummy is tired today," or "Mummy is sorry for shouting at you, but sometimes adults have bad moods, too." Years ago, they might have grinned at me and felt some satisfaction that they had worn me down. Now, they have empathy and compassion, and ask if they can do anything. They tell me it's OK to be sad or angry sometimes.

I'm sure you've all had a friend break down or complain about their kids and then later apologise about it. When this happens, I always take care to say that parenting in isolation is one of the most dangerous and lonely things we can do. A week, a day or sometimes just a few hours without adult contact can make our parenting troubles seem monumental. When we talk about our challenges, bounce ideas off each other, and share our stories, we start to feel human again. All it takes is a text message, quick chat, coffee or Facebook catch up.

This is one of my favourite parenting quotes, that makes me laugh when the shit is hitting the fan: "Don't compare yourself to other mothers. We are all losing our shit… some women just hide it better than others."

I am a hider trying to reform. I look like I have my shit together. Sometimes that's true. And often, it's not.

Jodie

One way I have learned to keep myself from breaking point is to exercise. I try to exercise daily, even if it means getting up early, or setting up a child next to me with paint and paper and a plea to let me have twenty minutes. On the days I do, it makes a profound difference to my patience, tolerance and general levels of happiness. When I say exercise, I mean hard, sweaty exercise. The more time I can get on the treadmill in a week, the better a parent I am.

I've never been a great exerciser and certainly not a runner, but I was losing my mind after a disturbing series of events with one of the kids. My husband could see I was struggling. He saw me drink whisky after I've barely had a drink for years. He drove up the driveway one day with a treadmill, hauled it into the garage, and set it up. I was gratefully annoyed. I didn't want a treadmill, and was sure this would get no use.

I thanked him and let him get excited about all the functions and features. Tentatively, a few days later, I found some old exercise clothes and hopped on. I walked, then jogged really slowly, and then ran. What I soon realised was that with every step, I was letting go of some of the struggles we had, my shoulders were dropping down, my back was relaxing. It felt amazing.

Then my husband bought a fight mannequin. He's called Bob. After I run to Beyoncé, I go and hit him for a couple more songs. The sweat drips down my face and I feel awesome. The endorphins last for hours afterwards, and there's little else that feels as good as this.

The treadmill saved my sanity and is now a regular feature of my day-to-day life. I am slightly obsessed, and it's the best obsession I've ever had.

◆　◆　◆

Another slightly curious sanity saver I use is Instagram-escapism. When times are tough, I will stalk the pages of what I call "Kinsfolk mothers". They look like they have such simple lives. Their children are dressed in linen, their surfing partners have man buns, they spend their days eating fruit on the beach, and in their spare time they write blogs that become bestselling novels or run cooking empires or create ethical fashion lines from recycled offcuts.

They rarely have teenagers but, if they do, they are a vision of creativity: making movies, becoming photographers, writing teenage fiction, winning prizes. I see no stories of troublemaking friends, self-harm, psychologists, or wanting to belong in a world that's fickle. I see no stories of fighting over homework, messy rooms, or endless assignments. I see no tales of full-time working office parents. The "business travel" they post about is to meet "friends" with complementary businesses in forests and fields for Insta-worthy picnics, not leaving the home before dawn to go to non-Insta-worthy meetings with people in suits in beige offices.

I use them to escape. I don't begrudge them their lives, nor do I really believe they are fully represented by their posts. They make me feel like life can be simple, pared back. Their pretty lives provide some respite from my beloved but often messy family life.

If I used my Instagram account now, I'd post pictures and you'd think my life was perfect: a beautiful rainbow family with a stay-at-home dad and working mum. How modern. How perfect. And it is – for the ten seconds it took to snap and post that photo.

◆　◆　◆

A final sanity saver that has multiple benefits: when life gets really tough, I clean. The cupboards that are full of junk get a massive sorting-out every few months. Whenever I'm giving the cupboards the side-eye and thinking about doing something, I remember that soon enough, my body will be possessed by such a strong urge to declutter, that I don't need to conjure the energy for it now.

Tammie

I thought I was a pretty calm person. I took things in my stride; I was rarely flustered or overly-angry about anything. We had two little girls: the first, an angel; the second, a girl who taught me a thing or two about tantrums. Then we adopted our boy, and my experience of tantrums went up a level – I'm talking *real* tantrums. Adult tantrums.

The first two months after bringing our boy home were blissful – the textbook honeymoon period. Then the endless sleepless nights and his difficult daytime behaviour began to take their toll on me. I found myself quick to snap. Around this time, I became pregnant with our fourth child. Suffice to say, I wasn't in the best mental state. I found myself demonstrating behaviours I had seen in small children with chronic ear infections: screaming, slamming things, stomping, banging. Noise, noise, noise. I released every bit of frustration through producing the loudest, scariest noises I could, whether they came from me or a cupboard door.

I was the exact opposite of the type of mother I thought I would be. I hated yelling and screaming. I never wanted to be like that. Ever. I was impatient, cranky, irrational and angry. Really, really angry.

I was angry that I wasn't me anymore. I was angry that I was tired. That I was overwhelmed. That my life had been taken over by this tiny little boy who didn't do what I wanted or expected him to do. Angry that I felt alone – not because I didn't have support, but because I had never required help with anything, and this wasn't supposed to be any different. I was an independent, capable person, who took on any challenge...

Add to the mix the fact that the scan and blood tests had shown that the baby I was still pregnant with was at high risk of chromosomal abnormalities. This prompted the kids and me to move from Dubai back to Australia, to continue the medical care there. With my husband still working in Dubai, we bought and renovated a house and moved in while I was pregnant. It was stupid to do all of that alone while pregnant and taking care of three children, one of whom was trying to adjust to a new family and who didn't sleep more than an hour at a time.

I went crazy. I *seemed* to function. People saw me, I socialised, I laughed and chatted. I provided everything the children needed (except a rational mother!). But this period in my life changed me. I was not just at breaking point; I had passed beyond it.

When the baby was born, I had endless love and patience for him. But I had little left for anyone else. I was angry at our adopted boy for turning me into a mess. I blamed him for me becoming everything

I hated. I resented him for taking away the kind, gentle mother I once was and replacing her with the cranky, yelling version that now existed.

Of course, there were many good times when he and I would be loving and kind and gentle with each other. I savoured these moments while they happened, and then quickly forgot they existed the next time he upset me.

I had always enjoyed yoga and being active, but now had zero time to myself. So, being someone with a strong leaning towards all things hippy, I started reading books about mindfulness: *The Tibetan Book of Living and Dying*, Deepak Chopra, *Buddhism for Mothers*, anything I could get my hands on to remind me how to be peaceful again. I would read, and feel inspired and calm – until one of the children did something that upset me!

This wasn't enough, though. I needed some time and space to allow my mental state to get back to a manageable place.

I had done a little bit of meditation here and there, but had never practiced it regularly. I was amazed when I started doing so. While I was putting the boys to sleep, I would sit on a mat in their room and meditate. This kept them calm because I was there, and it was so enjoyable that I didn't care how long it took them to fall asleep. This gave me time, a clear space, and helped me be a better person.

As soon as I was able to get some time on my own, I started going to yoga classes again. This allowed me to focus on my breath and my body for an hour and half at a time. This calmed me for the day. Sure, I would still get upset, but my mind wasn't jammed full like it used to be. Yoga and meditation bought me a little bit of space in my mind.

Now I know that if I don't manage to get to a yoga class, I need to go for a long walk in nature, consciously focusing on my breath and taking the time to be grateful for everything around me. I have introduced the children to meditation, and one of my favourite things to do is listen to a guided meditation with the boys before they go to sleep.

For Co-Parents: Keeping a Marriage or Partnership Together

When things with the kids are going really badly for a really long time, your relationship with your partner becomes just about the last thing you have the time and energy for.

When you're surviving dark times, you end up spending very little time together as you divide and conquer with the kids, giving each other breaks from the tyranny that can be parenthood some days.

You might have differences in opinion on parenting methods. You might judge each other's parenting. You might channel your unhappiness with the kids into dissatisfaction with your partner. You might be frustrated by how hard adoptive parenting is. You might have thought this would be easier.

Some of us have sailed too close to the wind with our marriages. Threatened to leave. Wanted to leave. Unable to see that the challenges we faced were very much to do with the kids and very little to do with us. You've heard of people who have had a baby to try and save their relationship. Anyone who adopts a child for the same reason is on a hiding to nothing. Adoptive parenting has brought intensive, explosive stress some of the time, and low-level stress much of the time. That wears you down.

When we had a violent child, it took its toll on me, my husband, and our marriage. I felt my husband was not focused on my welfare at all, that he didn't "protect me" enough, and I distinctly remember late one night, after another violent session, telling him I couldn't cope and I was going to leave. This is hard to imagine if you have not been through it. I am no weakling; in fact, I'm self-reliant and strong. But the cracks in our family were enormous and, given that her violence was directed towards me, it seemed sensible that I remove myself. I didn't want to – I adore the kids and my husband – but I didn't want this same thing to happen every few nights and I certainly didn't want the other kids to grow up in a violent home.

Keeping your partnership intact and healthy is vital. It is worth investing your time and energy into, even when things are horrible.

◆　◆　◆

Here are our tried and true suggestions for coping as a couple:

◊　You might have had the day from hell with a difficult child. If you've got a partner, you might later try to explain your frustration to them as they walk in from work. Your examples can make you sound ridiculous and trite. *She looked at me funny. She dropped her water.* Ensure your working partner spends enough one-on-one time with your child to understand the patterns, so that they can empathise with you properly. Otherwise, there can be months or years where you don't fully understand what each other is dealing with.

◊　If you are the primary carer and have a co-parent, sometimes you really want them to walk in the door and take over, to do the thinking for you. Often they're cautious, afraid to upset the natural order of things. You need to discuss this and agree that you are both able to call the shots – you aren't the head parent. That role doesn't exist.

◊ One of the best habits you can create as a new family is to get the kids to bed as early as physically possible. This gives you some time together. Some days, this gives you the space to let off steam if you've had a bad parenting day. The simple act of listening will make the world of difference.

◊ Work hard to see yourselves as individuals, with hobbies and interests of your own. Encourage each other to take some time to spend as you choose. Don't bitch and moan about being left with the kids; allow each other that. Live up to your commitments to each other. Having an interest or two also lets you feel like you've something to speak about beyond the kids.

◊ Spend time alone, just the two of you. In the early days, with a new family forming, it can be hard to get time alone. But you don't need to leave the kids. In fact, we recommend it's best *not* to leave the kids in the early days, if you can avoid it. This allows them to build trust that you are there and will continue to be there, much faster. Be practical, and find ways to enjoy each other's company once the kids have gone down. Watch a film or box sets together, have a bath together, play scrabble, or have one of you cook dinner for the other. As the kids become more settled and attached, take the time to head out together for a couple of hours here and there. If you don't have someone to help out close by, invest the time and energy in finding a good babysitter. I've always struggled with this – I knew my kids would run rings around a hired babysitter. Then we found a lady who works in drug and alcohol rehab, and I knew we were set!

◊ If you're having a serious issue with the kids, take the time to discuss it and strategise together, before jumping straight into problem-solving mode.

◊ Don't overschedule your lives, and make sure you have time together as a family. We deliberately keep our weekends quite free, meaning we can stay in our pajamas and lounge around the house, go for a picnic, have a walk, release and relax. Trying to jam lots of activities into the weekend is something we don't want to do. This also helps with bonding the family unit.

◈   Try to remember your physical relationship. There is nothing like sex to remind you of your pre-children connection. You feel like an adult when you make an effort here, even if it's only now and then.

◈   Always show the kids a united front. Let them know that you're a team. Even if you aren't happy with a decision or approach, try to wait until the kids aren't in earshot to discuss it. Defend each other to the kids: "Please don't speak to my wife like that."

◈   When you are chatting to each other, discuss the child's behaviour in earshot of the child. Describe the behaviour respectfully and without emotion, wonder what's causing it, and discuss strategies. This shows your child that you're working together, and that they can't divide and conquer.

◈   A trusted counsellor seen both together and separately can be helpful. Calm conversations happen in front of therapists – if you don't have that third person, you'll scream and swear. This also can be an efficient use of time as you can break a cycle that would otherwise drag on for weeks, when you never get to speak with each other until you're falling asleep, exhausted at the end of the day.

Fix You: Healthy Detachment

I went to see a psychologist to discuss how I was dealing with my son's various odd behaviours. She posed many questions and, after a while, asked why I felt like I needed to fix my son.

This puzzled me. We discussed it further. She told me that I could never undo the damage wrought during his first year of life. I could never fill that hole and make life perfect for him. I couldn't "fix" him.

It was one of those moments when someone says something that resonates so deeply in your soul as your truth, that you break. I cried and cried and cried as I realised how hard I had been trying to make everything OK for this child. I wanted to fix him, to make him whole again; I wanted the neglect, the abandonment, the feelings of worthlessness to go away. I wanted him to feel wanted and cared for and loved. I wanted him to be well adjusted and well behaved.

He will never be fixed. He will know that he has a family that loves him and cares for him and will teach him to care for himself, but he will always have funny little behaviours and reactions that make him who he is, because of where he has been.

I remind myself of this constantly. I can get frustrated when he zones out, or when he doesn't remember things, or when he panics about missing out on something. These are things I have spoken to him about time and time again. These are things that, no matter how hard he tries, he can't seem to shift. Maybe they will improve as he gets older; maybe they are here to stay.

I have to remind myself not to get too hung up on these things. To let go, relax about the little things. To remind him of things without getting so consumed by whether or not he is doing them.

Lots of books talk about healthy detachment, and that is exactly what I try to do: detach, just a little. Not love him any less, just back off and release that intense need for him to fit into the "perfect kid" category. Detach just enough to let him be, to not make myself mad with trying to modify so many of his behaviours.

Acceptance of the Children You Have

It's common wisdom that children are our greatest teachers. This is never more true than with adopted children. It can be a slow process to accept what your children teach you, as we initially try to reshape, rehash, and remould them into who we thought they would be.

At some point, if you're lucky, you'll have a flash of realisation that they are truly, truly hard-wired to be their own person. This acknowledgement brings clarity and peace when you realise your job is largely about accepting them. This acceptance makes it so much easier to be a decent, tolerant, loving parent to your child.

We started out totally open-armed and open-hearted, ready to accept our children as they were, just as we were counselled to do, and our feelings were genuine. I realise now that, beneath the surface, I believed that with ample time, love and attention, I'd mould our kids to be more and more like I thought I wanted them to be. I wanted them to be happy, interesting, hard-working, honest, committed to school, sensible, funny, and so on. Surely if we modelled these things, they would absorb these qualities by osmosis?

This underlying intention lived in me for many years. I didn't realise it was there. I never questioned that this was the future state for the kids, that we'd get there eventually.

One of the kids has suffered from anxiety and depression at times. I was the world's most annoying mother by my listening and empathising, but ultimately thinking she could get through it, that *we* could get through it, with positivity and optimism. Now, with a few more years under my belt, I'm embarrassed by that naïve "Mrs-Fix-It" attitude I had towards mental illness. I have now accepted that this child will have periods of sadness that I can't fix. What I can do, though, is keep a close eye on her so I know she is safe, ask her where she is on a scale of one to ten, and ensure she has excellent professional support. I can step back and accept this as part of who she is.

Acceptance is a peaceful thing, but you'd be ill-advised to accept everything you see in any child. You need to choose what you'll fight for, and let the less important things slide.

A couple of our kids hate school. This is hard for us as parents, as we both loved learning – in fact, we still love learning, and read often and widely. Unless we insist on regular reading at night, they will never choose to pick up a book for fun. Again, we accept this as part of the fabric that makes these two up. But you need to choose your battles and be thoughtful about your focus. We know that the kids' overall learning and education are vastly improved by regular reading, so while we accept the kids aren't into it, we still enforce it.

I used to worry whether the kids had done their homework, taken it to school, prepared for their test, or rehearsed their speech. My worry was based on my personal approach of doing things as requested, on time, and well. I thought that my example of thinking and planning ahead would eventually rub off, and the sense of responsibility I felt would transfer to the kids – that I'd pass on the flame, so to speak. Over a decade later, I'm still waiting!

Instead, we try to set up good habits around school – regular homework time, enquiries into what's due, an eager ear and advice if they're preparing a speech. But ultimately, we let them wear the responsibility. If they don't want to put in a lot of effort, we'll let them bear the consequences. We praise them a lot when they work hard and earn good marks, but the pleasure does seem fleeting to them. When they haven't worked hard, and get the results justified by the lack of work, we don't sugar-coat it. We'll discuss it calmly and without an agenda, without shouting or judgement. We'll ask the kids what they think they can do differently next time. But *they* own the work and the consequences, and it's a blessed relief.

Honesty is a quality that is most important to us as a family: we ensure the kids know that telling the truth will always improve outcomes, that we value the truth and expect it. We will put in the hard yards around promoting honesty and punishing lies. We outlined our approach to honesty and lies in the Behavioural Challenges section.

When you start on your adoptive parenting journey, it's helpful, in a quiet moment, to consider your family values: which battles will you fight, and which will you take an easier stance on? Sure, get your family values printed on a poster for your lounge room if that helps, but at the very least, reiterate your expectations with your kids in both the calm and the storm.

Epilogue

At the start of this book, we said we'd cover the harder parts of adoptive parenting. We want this book to help you, to save you the years of trial and error we've gone through, to make you feel like you're not alone and that others have gone through similar trials.

We thought it would be a fitting end to this book to tell you a little more about where we are, a decade after becoming adoptive families.

Our kids are mostly in a pretty good place. We understand them better, and we're helping them to better understand themselves. Our goal is still to build healthy, happy and resilient kids. That is a lifelong project, really, isn't it? Some of them are still going through issues, but the issues are shifting and changing, and that in itself is progress. We are dealing with things methodically and thoughtfully. The high intensity work we did for many years is abating. We enjoy the children far more today than we did years ago. Having children is a lottery – even more so with adopted children – and it can be an absolute delight to see how they develop and who they become.

Learning remains one of the hardest challenges for us. While it's appropriate and, in fact, essential to deal with trauma and attachment issues first, helping most of our children with learning issues remains a big part of our day-to-day lives.

As parents, we are much less stressed than when we started out. We promise you it gets easier. It's easier for several reasons – the kids' issues have reduced over time, we understand them better, and we are better equipped at making ourselves calmer and more resilient.

There have been hideous, horrible days in our parenting journey. But these have been far outweighed by wonderful days, by seeing the kids self-regulate or sleep or get on top of their food issues. By seeing their pride as they learn something new. By exploring the world together. By them telling us they love us for the first time.

We say adoptive parenting is for the full of heart, the "lionhearts", not the faint of heart. We are so grateful for the opportunity to be adoptive parents.

82938392R00192

Made in the USA
Lexington, KY
07 March 2018